MAKING
COMMITTEES
WORK

Also by Mack Tennyson . . .

Church Finances for People Who Count

MAKING
COMMITTEES
WORK

MACK TENNYSON

ZondervanPublishingHouse
Academic and Professional Books
Grand Rapids, Michigan

A Division of HarperCollins*Publishers*

MAKING COMMITTEES WORK
Copyright © 1992 by Mack Tennyson

Requests for information should be addressed to:
Zondervan Publishing House
Academic and Professional Books
Grand Rapids, Michigan 49530

Library of Congress Cataloging-in-Publication Data

Tennyson, Mack.
    Making committees work / Mack Tennyson.
        p.   cm.
    ISBN 0-310-58471-X
    1. Church meetings. 2. Church committees. I. Title.
    BV652.15.T46   1992   92-11388
    254'.6—dc20   CIP

All Scripture quotations, unless otherwise noted, are taken from THE HOLY
BIBLE: NEW INTERNATIONAL VERSION (North American Edition),
copyright © 1973, 1978, 1984 by the International Bible Society. Used by
permission of Zondervan Bible Publishers.

Cover design by The Church Art Works
Interior design by Louise Bauer

Printed in the United States of America

92 93 94 95 96 97 / ML / 10 9 8 7 6 5 4 3 2 1

To my three blonde sweethearts:

Sarah Tennyson
Rebekah Tennyson
Anna Tennyson

Contents

Acknowledgments

Many thanks to my two helpers:
Randy Blyth and Cathy Morris.

Chapter 1

The Spirited Meeting

It is 11:00 P.M. The board meeting is dragging on. The members are making an important decision, but Pastor Jim's mind wanders. This would not be so bad, except that he is chairing the committee.

The church board is choosing the sanctuary's carpet color. One group wants a bright rust color. The other wants a light beige. The beige group thinks the red looks too cheap, and the rust group thinks the beige group is crazy to put white in a public place: "It'll be dirty in a week."

Brother Boyce raises his hand, and Pastor Jim reluctantly nods for him to speak. He knows what is coming. Boyce is a wonderful soul who speaks without breathing: "I believe that we need a brighter color than the rust color and the beige is just fine, but who can tell for sure whether it will hold up under all the traffic that we have in the sanctuary, I am sure that it would look good in my house, well, for that matter the rust would look good in my house even though I wouldn't have it because I personally believe that it is too flashy, I am not saying that those who want it are too flashy, I am just saying that it is too flashy for . . ."

Pastor Jim scans the room. Most members look brain dead. Brother Boyce is famous for his soliloquies. The longest that Pastor Jim ever timed was twenty minutes. Brother Boyce goes on and on and on and . . .

Brother Ebenezer interrupts. He prides himself as a down-to-brass-tacks, no beating-around-the-bush type of person. He says, "That's the dumbest thing I've ever heard. Who cares whether the red or white carpet looks good in your house? I move we don't get carpet and use linoleum instead. It lasts longer, and nothing is prettier than shiny linoleum. We once had linoleum. Linoleum was good enough when I was a kid, and it is good enough now!"

Pastor Jim immediately shifts from being partially asleep to a state of high anxiety. There has never been a church board meeting without an argument with Brother Ebenezer.

Pastor Jim chooses his words carefully. "I agree with you a little, Brother Ebenezer. I prefer to keep the old carpet one more year and use the money for outreach. But our very last vote was for buying new carpet. So I don't think opening it up again is okay."

"We never discussed linoleum. I say we should vote again. Linoleum is a good idea."

Pastor Jim says, "All who favor using linoleum, raise your hand."

At first only Brother Ebenezer raises his hand, then his wife timidly joins him. But linoleum is voted down. Finally everyone gets tired, and since Pastor Jim does not want new carpet, they all go home.

Walking home, Pastor Jim looks at the stars and wonders, "Why do we make decisions in meetings? Why couldn't I visit the sick or do counseling or do anything? I hate meetings! I don't remember Jesus in committees. I can't see him saying, 'I hear a motion that we go heal the sick by

10

Galilee. Is there a second?' Then again, I'm not Jesus. What would Jesus do with Brother Boyce and Brother Ebenezer? Sometimes I wish I could punch Brother Ebenezer's nose. Is the Holy Spirit in this? I thought I was Spirit-led, not committee-led!"

The stars leave the questions unanswered. Pastor Jim is too tired to care.

MEETING THEOLOGY

Pastor Jim raises some interesting questions about meetings. Everywhere in Christianity, groups are making decisions in meetings. The Presbyterian Church is making big decisions about church members' sexuality, and a little church is making little decisions about painting the Sunday school classrooms. Because Christians spend so much time in meetings, it seems we need a Meeting Theology.

Any Meeting Theology must answer two questions: (1) How did Bible characters make church decisions? (2) How does the Holy Spirit fit into group decision making?

Church Decisions

The Bible often speaks of individual decision making, as in Joshua 24:15: "Then choose for yourselves this day whom you will serve." Scripture rarely shows groups making decisions. Americans view democracy as a God-given right, but defending that position solely from the Bible is difficult.

Throughout the Old Testament, leaders issued decisions by decree. The patriarchs firmly ruled their families. The judges ruled Israel by the decisions God gave them. The kings ruled by military and inherited right. Advisers gave counsel, but the decision always came from one person.

One exception may be observed in Moses' appointing the elders as assistants. However, these elders functioned as sole decision makers dealing with mundane matters. They used their authority to make decisions that relieved their overworked leader. Scripture does not say that they were a decision-making group; they individually attended to the people under their care.

The Gospels relate how Jesus led the disciples as one who made the decisions for the group. The group members followed, even when they opposed the direction he was taking. The people nearly stoned Jesus and his group on a recent visit to Jerusalem. Jesus directed his followers to return, even though the group thought that going back was unwise and that they would be following him to their death. Yet they respected their leader and followed him (Matt. 16:21–23; Mark 10:33–34).

Only the book of Acts shows groups making decisions. Church decision making appears three times. The first time was after Jesus' death, but before the Spirit descended (Acts 1). To replace Judas, the disciples set up a guideline: The person must have followed Jesus from his baptism until his resurrection. They proposed two men, Joseph and Matthias. They prayed for guidance, cast lots, and thereby decided. This decision-making process blended intellect and supernatural involvement.

If it were not for the Holy Spirit, we might still make decisions by casting lots. But after the Holy Spirit's outpouring, group decisions became more democratic. Acts 15 relates the Bible's clearest example of group decisions.

The apostles and elders had to decide whether it was necessary to circumcise the Gentiles who turned to the Christian faith. First they debated the issue (v. 7). They grounded their debate in logic tempered by the miracles Peter and Paul reported (v. 12). They reviewed their heritage (v. 10) and Scripture's teaching (v. 16). They also expressed raw opinion (v. 19).

After the debate, the Bible relates, "They decided . . ." (v. 22). It does not say how the group decided. Was there a majority vote or a unanimous decision? The important thing is that the apostles and elders made a decision that set out a reasonable action, and then they acted. The committee wrote a letter that started like this: "The apostles and elders, your brothers, To the Gentile believers . . ." (v. 23). Imagine the process they must have gone through to craft that letter!

Peter may have said, "We need some introductory words about why we are writing."

Paul says, "No, get right to the point. Start by saying, 'It seemed good to us not to burden you with anything beyond the following requirements.'"

James says, "You fellows have more experience writing than I, but it seems that we should say that the Holy Spirit helped with the decision."

Paul says, "Okay, let's say, It seemed good to the Holy Spirit and to us not to burden you with anything beyond the following requirements: . . .'" (v. 28).

They continued in the same manner until they finished the letter.

The most startling thing about the whole process is that they met, discussed, and decided. Then they wrote a letter stating their decision as the Holy Spirit's decision: "It seemed good to the Holy Spirit. . . ." *Today's English Version* says, "The Holy Spirit and we have agreed. . . ." The participants depicted their group decision as a word from the Holy Spirit. This gives today's committees some hope.

THE HOLY SPIRIT AND DECISION MAKING

Can people who sit around discussing and then voting really be God's agents in the twentieth-century church? It seems that God could have found a better way. Why no more mystical wall writing or talking donkeys?

Developing a Spirit-directed theology of life can be easy. Seeing the Spirit working in an individual's life can be easy. Seeing him guide a person can be easy. But doing the same things for a group seems hard. Are we left to our own resources?

The Spirit leads a church the same way he leads an individual. Think how he has guided you. Think about struggling with a decision. Flashes of great Spirit-filled inspiration are rare. But as time goes by, alternatives come into focus. Some become more logical. The direction becomes clear, and you have peace about your decision. An outsider sees you make a rational decision just as everyone else does. You weigh the alternatives using logic, experience, and acquired knowledge.

The non-Christian uses the same decision-making process, because God built this into the human brain. But for the nonbeliever the process lacks the vital link that makes it great. The Spirit-filled Christian follows the same process as everyone else, except that God gives wisdom and leads the way. To make decisions using logic, experience, and additional knowledge is God given. Linking it with the Holy Spirit makes it divine.

The same reality exists when groups make decisions. A public school board makes decisions based on its best wisdom, using logic, experience, and the available data. The church board uses the same God-given process, but adds an extra, Spirit-filled vitality.

Churches are operated on this premise: A Spirit-filled group makes more reliable decisions than a Spirit-filled individual. A group can find God's will for a church better than an individual. Why is this? Perhaps the checks and balances that groups offer are a safety device.

We have all seen Christians get excited about an idea that they are certain was given by the Spirit. They work on the idea, invest time and money in its fulfillment, but finally it flops.

Brother Chuck had a bright idea that he said came to him as he was about to fall asleep one night. Certain that the Spirit had given him the brainstorm, Chuck stayed up all night to work on the project. This was his idea: As a means of outreach, the church would run seminars on personal finance. Chuck developed course material, brochures, and advertisements and arranged for a meeting place. He enlisted helpers to greet participants and hand out material. On the first night no one showed up, not even his own church members.

Rather than being Spirit-led, Chuck may have simply been suffering from the thrill that comes with having a good idea. This happens less often with a group than with individuals. The Spirit must move several minds, so there are some checks on the process.

Even with checks and balances, a system is not perfect. We see this when two church groups pray about a decision and subsequently make conflicting decisions.

A subcommittee may work for hours on a decision. The members are confident that God is guiding their actions. But when their decision goes to the higher committee, it is rejected as unwise and voted down. How can this happen? Was the Spirit working in one group and not in the other?

This kind of conflict arises among groups for the same reason that it happens with individuals. God's goal is to develop the best character in us. Individual decisions do not have primary importance. The Spirit inspired Chuck to run the seminars. But the Spirit's purpose was, it seemed to Chuck, humility.

One Spirit-filled group votes down a second Spirit-filled group's decision. Perhaps the Spirit is teaching the first group humility or is seeking to develop patience. The Spirit has many more priorities than merely having committees make decisions.

Committees and Faith

The Bible clearly teaches that we are to yield to the authority of employers, spouses, and governments:

> Everyone must submit himself to the governing authorities, for there is no authority except that which God has established. The authorities that exist have been established by God. Consequently, he who rebels against the authority is rebelling against what God has instituted, and those who do so will bring judgment on themselves (Rom. 13:1–2).

Respecting authority is following established leadership even if it seems wrong. This is not blind faith, but rather, faith that God works things out in spite of the leader's error.

Respecting authority is difficult if the authority resides in a committee. We can easily respect a wise teacher's position or another person's great power or prominence, but it is difficult to respect a church board.

Church members must submit to the governing board's

decisions. This does not mean committees are infallible. It means that God honors our respect for the authority and may work out matters to our satisfaction in spite of the board's errors.

What does it mean, practically speaking, to respect authority? Suppose the youth minister asks the board, "I want to take the kids to Three Flags amusement park. I need the church van and about a hundred dollars for expenses. We will be gone for two days."

The church board hotly debates the trip. Brother Ebenezer says, "I don't think amusement parks are fitting places for children. It overexcites their nervous systems, and after spinning around like that they cannot appreciate spiritual things."

Others speak against the trip. Some speak in favor of it. Back and forth it goes until finally the board votes against the outing. The youth minister and others who favor the trip could rebel against the committee's authority. They could tell the hopeful kids that although the board voted against it, the group will make the trip anyway. The kids could get their parents to give them the money, and the youth minister could take them on her day off.

The fruits of the rebellion are obvious. The youth minister faces a decision of the will: Either she could change the trip so the idea is more palatable to the board, or she could strive with each member and hope for a change of vote. But open rebellion reaps a terrible harvest.

THE POINT OF THE BOOK

Two premises form the basis of this book. First, *Christian committees exist to find God's will*. This book develops this theme through the chair's role. The chair leads this spiritual search and weaves it into the members' role. The members prayerfully seek his will and are the means by which God communicates his will. The agenda allows ample time for the searching. The meeting room is a place appropriate for conducting the search. This first premise weaves through every part of the meeting.

The Spirited Meeting

The book's second premise is that people are more important than meetings. A Christian spends much time in meetings, so committees do more than just make decisions. Committees also exist to grow and to show the fruit of the Spirit. God worries more about how the chair treats the members than whether the meeting runs efficiently. How members treat Brother Ebenezer concerns God more than which carpet color is selected. The agenda and meeting place must show respect for individuals. For many Christians, meetings are their only mission field.

Chapter 2

We Must Stop Meeting Like This

"I am not getting in trouble. No, not in this meeting!" Church meetings are making Pastor Jim sick, but not because he dislikes meetings. Until now he has enjoyed the groups socially. He has felt good about planning the work of God in Shulerville. But recently meetings have gotten him in trouble. As he drives into the church parking lot he decides that this is one church meeting in which he will avoid the debate. He will simply chair the meeting, remain completely impartial, and stay out of trouble.

The agenda is the purchase of a new piano. One faction thinks the church needs a grand piano; the other wants an electronic keyboard—not a cheap one, but one that costs two thousand dollars. The latter group believes the versatility makes an electronic keyboard the more attractive choice.

Pastor Jim prefers the keyboard, mainly because the

piano the church has now is always out of tune. The temperature swings in the sanctuary are hard on a tuned piano. But Jim has decided that he does not really care what the church does. So tonight he is keeping his mouth shut with the thought, "Just chair the committee and keep quiet."

Surprisingly, the meeting goes just the way Pastor Jim planned. One group presses for the piano; the other argues for the keyboard. Brother Ebenezer alone forms a third faction, one that could be called the "what's wrong with the piano we have?" bloc.

Brother Ebenezer says, "I don't think anything is wrong with the piano we have. Wouldn't it be better to save the money and use it in evangelism? What do you think, Pastor?"

This sounds innocent enough. But Pastor Jim sees it for what it is—a trap. It is a trap well baited for Jim's ego. Hardly anyone can resist expressing an opinion when directly asked for it. Pastor Jim says, "My opinion is not important. You folks must live with your decision—and pay for it." He adds the last comment for Brother Ebenezer's benefit.

The discussion goes on for two hours. It is good that Jim avoids the debate. Twice he calms down members who have become overexcited. If he aligns with either group, they could accuse him of using his position of authority to sway the decision his way.

Sister Sue leads the grand piano faction. After two hours of championing her cause, she surprises everyone with the admission, "Keeping a piano tuned is very hard unless you keep the temperature constant. So if we get a grand piano we must heat the sanctuary all winter and air conditioner all summer." This is unfeasible and virtually impossible. The members built the sanctuary in 1842. To heat or cool it everyday costs a fortune. So the group chooses the electronic keyboard.

As Pastor Jim leaves the parking lot, he thinks, "Why couldn't I have made the decision? They argued for two hours, strained some feelings, and came to the same decision I would have made. Why waste all that time?"

The fact is, the board did several things more important

than choose a piano. First, it gave the church members exercise in their Christian graces. Also, the people who will pay for the keyboard made the decision, making fund-raising easier. Indeed, from Pastor Jim's viewpoint the meeting concerned fund-raising more than choosing the piano. Finally, allowing wider involvement gave the members broader ownership in other, more important church activities.

You would enjoy writing this chapter. It deals with a favorite topic of conversation during bathroom and coffee breaks: Meetings waste time. Why do we meet like this? What good do meetings do? This chapter reviews the good things and the bad things, the benefits and the detriments, of committees.

GOOD THINGS

To write good things about meetings is almost like speaking well of Adolf Hitler. Everyone loves to bad-mouth meetings. No one speaks well of them. Most people see them as evil. However, there are several things that meetings accomplish that cannot be easily achieved any other way.

Character Development

The most important benefit is not the most obvious: Meetings provide a good place to practice the Christianity we preach. The Christian fruits are love, joy, peace, patience, kindness, goodness, faithfulness, gentleness, and self-control (Gal. 5:22–23). Faking these fruits for a church service or a church fellowship dinner or when working for the poor is easy. But faking them in church meetings is hard. The next time you feel that you are wasting time in a meeting, think about the character you are developing.

Meetings also give us an opportunity to attune to our fellow members' spiritual problems. God calls ministers to spread the gospel and feed the flock. Sadly, many ministers spend much unnecessary time in meetings. Some deal with this conflict between the ministry and meetings by seeing meetings as an evil that may finally lead to ministry. Others deal with the conflict by seeing meetings as a ministry in itself.

Suppose the committee is buying a piano. You can justify the time spent in the meeting two ways. One way is to say, "If we have a good piano, we can have a better worship service, That better worship service brings people closer to God." The other way is to say, "That is true. But my main purpose is helping people develop the Christian fruits. I do this by my example and by direct encouragement. Meetings give me a chance to do this. In meetings, I see members in a more honest light. It is better than seeing them in a home visit or shaking hands as they leave the church."

If selecting a piano is the only reason that the minister is meeting, he could spend his time better elsewhere. Try applying this to the extent that you do not care about the committee's purpose or outcome. Simply see meeting as a chance to shepherd and serve your members. This is the real answer to boring meetings.

Increased Involvement

With the spiritual benefits of meetings come several not-so-spiritual aspects. People are more willing to carry out some project when they have helped to make decisions about it. This is obvious in matters such as youth programs. Youth workers take the kids where they themselves like to go, and they do not take the kids where they do not like to go. So if others, such as the church board, sets up the youth program, the events will not happen. This connection between workers and decision making is obvious and crucial.

There is a less obvious connection. People who make decisions in one sphere commit more to the total church program. So it is wise not to load committees with older or more committed church members. Always include some new or less-committed members. This strategy broadens the base of involvement and therefore of commitment. Watch the changes that result.

Improved Decisions

Groups generally make better decisions than individuals. Admitting this is difficult. This is a general rule, and there are exceptions. However, the saying about two heads being better than one holds true, whether in a Christian or a secular setting. Chapter 1 considered how the decisions made by a group seeking to know and to do God's will are usually more reliable than individual decisions. A group works with more expertise and information than an individual does.

Rarely does a church have a super expert with wisdom exceeding a committee's wisdom. Many church decisions are not all that complex. When information and interpersonal aspects are missing, church decisions become difficult. So expertise is not as important as information and "people skills."

Another reason groups make better decisions is that they have more information. The group members bring information from all over the church. No individual could ever know all that is happening. Several members collectively with their information pool can mold a better decision than an individual.

BAD THINGS

Such are the benefits! But it is more fun looking at a committee's detrimental aspects. You have probably experienced all these bad things and more.

Cost

Cost is perhaps the most obvious weakness. The next time you are meeting, calculate the cost. Estimate the members' hourly wages and add them up. Even if the church is not actually expending cash, this is still the meeting's hidden cost. Each member's time is worth that much in wages. Suppose a person is attending a meeting at a time when he or she would otherwise be on the job; the hours consumed constitute wages lost—wages that could be given to the church. So that is the church's cost. Another example:

Consider that everyone there could be delivering pizzas and giving the money to the church. In this light even the smallest meeting is "costing" the church hundreds of dollars.

Frustration

Think about your church's interpersonal troubles. Many situations began with someone's saying or doing something in a meeting. Meetings are emotional cauldrons and can stunt the growth of spiritual fruit. Emotions and pride run strong during meetings. Combine these with the pressures of decision making and it's no wonder that meetings can become a battleground. Rise above the strife with love, joy, peace, patience, kindness, goodness, faithfulness, gentleness, and self-control.

Wise church leaders handle problem meetings in a positive and nurturing way. Lead the group in developing spiritual fruit and avoid focusing on hurt feelings or careless comments. Here is an example:

The church musicians are meeting. Sister Cheryl says to Sister Joyce, "You don't know how to transpose music? It is so easy. Are you sure you don't know how to transpose music?" Her tone rings with vanity. Your first urge is to run to Sister Joyce's defense: "Sister Cheryl, transposing music is not easy. How can you be so vain?" However, your goal is to help each member grow spiritually. So you nurture the members and ignore the argument.

Try to say something like, "This is a good chance to work on patience. Sister Cheryl, I know you want the church service just right. Sister Joyce, I know that it is hard to hear someone talk so bluntly about your playing. Your first reaction must be to quit playing for the church. Now is a chance for you both to work on patience."

I know this sounds unnatural, but it makes good sense. Work toward building spiritual fruit instead of focusing on the surface problems.

Real Work

Another detriment of meetings is that they do not accomplish real work. *People* do real work. Meetings just talk about real work. Unfortunately people get confused about this. This confusion causes problems. People think that if they are meeting they are somehow making a contribution. Not until the meeting turns into finished action is God's work advanced. Meetings come to fruition in people's doing things afterward. For example, a meeting on the subject of evangelism is not evangelism. Evangelism happens only after someone goes out and evangelizes.

Bad Decisions

Meetings lead to bad decisions. This may sound like a contradiction with the benefit of "improved decisions." However, groups make bad decisions differently from the way individuals make them. Groups use compromise to reach a decision. There is a group selecting church carpeting. One faction wants red carpet, the other wants light yellow. Either color looks good. The opinions represent merely minor differences in taste. However, the compromise color is orange (yellow and red), and it looks ugly. Often compromises give us something worse than either option.

Another reason for bad decisions is that committee members may lack accountability. A person gives more care to a decision made alone than to a group decision, because the owner receives both the good and the bad credit. With a committee, credit or blame is spread over all the members. So if a decision goes well, no one gets much credit; if it goes poorly, no one gets much blame.

This means people give more thought and care than small groups, and small groups give more thought and care than large groups. In large groups we need to invite members to share their thoughts, because they are very likely to feel their participation has little effect on the outcome. We must prompt the members to contribute to the process.

MEETING ALTERNATIVES

Committees have negative aspects. They are expensive and frustrating. They can make bad decisions and lack accountability. How can we ensure obtaining the benefits of committees and avoiding the detriments?

Stop Them

Because groups lack accountability, some experts say only individuals, not committees, should make action-type decisions. Committees should still handle policy-type decisions. Suppose a church raises money for a new building. The question arises, "Where do we invest the money until we start the church building?"

In most cases church boards or finance committees make the decision about investments. That changes under the scheme whereby individuals make action decisions and committees set policy. With this approach, the finance committee sets the policy: Invest in Certificates of Deposit or Treasury Bills. Then the treasurer finds the best rate and determines the investment. The treasurer has complete liberty within the policy to make investments.

This approach is better. Since the treasurer is accountable for the decision, he puts good effort into searching for the best rate. It is unlikely that a group's effort will match the individual's effort.

It takes only a little imagination to see how this approach works in the youth program. The church board sets the budget and establishes a basic guideline: "All youth activities must have an outreach element." Then the youth director decides the program on his or her own.

With this scheme, church leaders always work to keep committees away from specific action decisions. They also give people who make action decisions some room to fail. They evaluate a person on general performance and not on specific decisions.

Round-Robin Letters

Round-robin letters are another way to avoid the bad things about committees. This kind of letter draws information and expertise from everyone without a meeting. Large groups find this strategy more appropriate than small groups do.

Suppose there is a problem. The church board votes that someone from the ministerial staff will be always on call. The way to cover the "call" is a sensitive issue. Senior ministers feel they should not be assigned as much as the younger ministers: "We have paid our dues. It is time the younger set carries the heavier load." The younger ministers feel that their families' demands suggest that the elder ministers should do more. The youth ministers feel that they have a specific constituency to whom they are on call. All this discussion is going on in a polite Christian way.

The board, believing that a schedule set autocratically would be unfair, charges the church administrator to untangle the problem. The senior pastor is apprehensive about a meeting that would allow everyone's feelings to be vented at once.

The administrator initiates the round-robin approach. The staff will communicate entirely through interoffice memos. The administrator gives the first instruction: "Write how you feel about taking call. Write as much as you like." She then gathers the responses, photocopies them for everyone, and sends them out with the next instruction: "After reading all the other responses, write anything you want about someone else's response or write more about your own response."

The administrator goes through several cycles, each one progressing toward a practical solution. Near the end she starts to send out the schedule and receive feedback.

Imagine going through such a process to choose the sanctuary carpet. Imagine not having a meeting at which people can carelessly hurt someone else's feelings. Imagine getting everyone's input without long speeches. .

26

This approach compels individual involvement. It avoids thoughtless bickering. It is expensive, because writing out the responses takes time. But meetings are expensive also. Consider that a meeting held to choose carpet might take two hours. By contrast, many round-robin responses can be written in two hours, and that time can be fit variously into busy individual schedules.

CONCLUSION

This chapter has reviewed the good and bad sides of meetings. It has looked at ways of doing without them. The next chapter surveys types of meetings and explains when each kind is appropriate.

Chapter 3

Types of Meetings

"What an emotional roller coaster! Last week it looked as if there were no problems with this project, and this week everything is going wrong!"

The situation does not deter Pastor Jim, but it does surprise him. This is how it happened. For the past two years Pastor Jim thought that the congregation needed a church school. He saw a church school as a long-lasting contribution he could make to the Shulerville Community Church. He was reluctant to push for it until he felt that he had firmly established his place in the church.

Over recent months he had been taking deliberate steps toward the founding of a church school. Finally he asked the board to set up a church school committee. As he had hoped, the board created a super committee of the leading members of the congregation. These were people whose years and wisdom set them apart as vital church leaders. Jim even put Brother Ebenezer on the committee with the thought, "If I can get all these people on my side, nothing will stop the school."

The committee met and surprised Pastor Jim with their willingness and eagerness to start a church school. They laid the plans, projected enrollment, and determined where classes would meet. "The Sunday school building has the classrooms. They just need some work. We can get the parents in on that. It is just a few evenings' work." The committee even outlined a budget. It covered every detail.

So Jim thought. Then he began talking to the parents. Every time he met with a parent, he eagerly laid out the group's plans. The parents' apathy shocked him. They were mildly in favor of the idea, but not enthusiastic. Jim thought they would be excited. Now he worries that the school will lack a student body large enough to make it work. What is going wrong?

The secret is, people like to plan the activities that affect them. Perhaps this is a hangover from the days of the Boston Tea Party: "No taxation without representation." No commitment without a stake. People must often be coaxed into supporting a project they do not plan.

Jim's error came from not using the type of meeting he needed to get the school going. He felt that if the major church leaders voted for something, this in itself would make it happen. So he formed a legislative-type group. He was wrong.

What Jim needed was an action-type group. The parents, not the church leaders, must make the school plans, because they are the ones who do the work. If they make the plans, they will support them.

MEETING TYPES

There are several meeting types. If we understand them, we can choose the right type for a specific purpose. The different types of meetings function differently. The meeting types are (1) action, (2) decision making, (3) information trading, (4) conflict resolution, and (5) governance.

Action Groups

Action groups are the most common type of meeting. They fulfill a specific task. This is their life cycle: We set them up; the members meet and decide how to do their task; they carry out the task; then they decide how well they did.

We organize them. This step is vital. A successful business skillfully blends the success factors: labor, capital, and raw materials. A successful shoe company needs people who know how to make and market shoes: This is the labor part. The company also needs equipment and buildings: This is the capital part. It needs leather, packaging, and so on: This is the material part.

Throwing these three elements together carelessly does not bring success. Too much capital or labor is costly and makes the company unprofitable. Too much raw material does the same thing. Having the skilled factory labor, but not the right raw materials is bad. The successful entrepreneur skillfully blends these things.

Some ministers see the church the same way and think of themselves as the church's spiritual entrepreneur. Suppose the church needs a program for the youth. The minister can make plans, promote the program, drive the van, watch the kids, and be the spiritual leader. Or he can bring the needed elements together. The successful church is one in which the minister blends the requirements necessary to get a job done. He can recruit good workers, line up some money, and get materials. After he assembles these components, he works to start the process. Once it begins, he is freed to start another program. The program can run without his constant care.

The workers make their plans and carry them out. They use the resources they or the minister generates. The group runs the youth program differently from the way the minister would do it himself. The program reflects the committee's personality. Good ministers like these results.

Leading an action meeting is different from leading other

types. The focus is getting the job done, so members' suggestions and plans must be concrete. One can do away with high theories about youth development. It is more a question of "Where are we going, and who is driving?" The decisions are very job-oriented. So let the group members make the decisions.

Group leaders whose style is too overbearing may find themselves alone because members do not sense ownership for the plan. They simply find other things more pressing. If they feel that they did the planning, they work harder at making the plans work.

Another trait of action groups is the way they make decisions. With action groups, majority rule is not good enough. Suppose the youth committee has ten members. Some prefer to take the kids to an amusement park, and the others think it is wrong. There is hot debate. Finally six vote for the amusement park trip. We should expect only the six to take the kids to the park. The other four will not feel a responsibility to carry out the plan.

Action groups must work toward consensus, that is, a situation in which there is overwhelming agreement and those who disagree do not feel their position too strongly. In action groups, do not expect hard work from members who do not help make the plans or who oppose the program.

A well-run action group must have a self-evaluation method. After the group decides what it is going to do, make a check list. List the outcomes that will show success and the results that will demonstrate failure. When you finish the project, go through the check list to see how well the project worked. This book devotes an entire chapter to the subject of evaluation.

Decision-making Groups

Decision-making groups decide the way the church will proceed on an issue, but they do not carry out the decision. Some examples of decision-making groups are the church nominating committee, the building committee, and the finance committee. They all follow certain steps: (1) They

31

clearly state the problem, (2) they identify the facts needed to make a good decision, (3) they gather the facts, (4) they work out the options, and (5) they decide among the options.

The church needs a new photocopier. The correct choice may be simple—the minister presents his favorite to the church board, and the board votes on it. However, the situation may be more complex than that. The copier may be used by the church school, so it will be hard to decide on the needed size. Don't expect the minister to take a risk and decide. That is unfair. The board should form a subcommittee, and it should select the right copy machine.

The copier committee must clearly state the problem: Which copier to get? They must identify the facts it needs: How much copying is required by the church and the school? Which copiers handle that output? What special features are needed on the copier? How much money is available for a copier? The list goes on.

Then the committee gathers the facts and begins stating options: any of three particular copiers could nicely handle the work load, and any can be either bought or leased. The committee then chooses among the options.

Think about this process before assembling the group. Choose people who know how to work through options and can make good decisions. But include some unseasoned group decision makers, for this will enable them to learn the process.

The group leader's job is to shepherd the group through these steps. A domineering leader blocks the process so that the best solution may be missed. Suppose the group leader thinks one option is best. He should reserve his opinion until the group has done its homework, developed options, and has matured in its thinking. A weak group leader, by contrast, fails to keep the group moving. The group gets little done, and members become angry. Often they choose an inferior option just to get a decision made.

Sometimes church leaders form a decision-making group even though they have a clear idea what they want done. Their purpose is to build support and validate their idea.

They do not really want the group to make a decision. This strategy usually backfires. Bringing together a supposedly decision-making group and stubbornly directing the decision is a mistake. It is far better to be honest and say, "I have an idea I want to sell you."

As with action groups, decision groups need more than a majority vote. The decision of a strongly divided group reveals itself as weak even if the majority support it. Sometimes, it is true, a simple "majority rules" may be the only way out of a serious dilemma. However, the committee should review widely split votes to see if the problem needs more work.

Information-trading Groups

The next type of meeting is information trading. Everyone contributes to the information pool, and everyone draws from it. Many church board meetings allow a place on the agenda for this. Each group reports what it is doing and talks about its concerns. The purpose is to let all the church leaders know what is going on so they can give counsel and help.

This type of committee can be larger than the other groups already described, and its membership can comprise a wide cross section of the congregation. Voting is not the focus. Informal answers are sought through the exchange of information and the discussion of problems.

An information-trading meeting requires leaders who inspire others to share information. The leader ascertains beforehand that there are enough problems to warrant a meeting. This can be difficult to discern, because sometimes the problem-sharing process brings to light even more problems. During the meeting the leader leads the process by drawing out the timid and managing the talkative.

Churches have all too often been the victims of a cheap trick. Someone disguises an information meeting as a decision-making meeting. A church leader—perhaps the pastor— has designed a new youth program he wants adopted. He could honestly say, "I have a new program that I think you will like. Let's meet and look at it. Let me try to show you the good things about it." Instead he says, "I want to meet with you, so we can decide what we want as a youth program."

The young people show up expecting to develop a youth program. Instead they end up seeing a performance by the pastor. Then to validate what he is doing, he calls for a vote. Often such a vote is meaningless.

This kind of deception reduces everyone's trust in the leader. The next time he really needs help in planning a program, no one will respond.

Conflict Resolution Groups

Sometimes churches must ignore conflict between members. The Bible admonishes us to talk out problems with those who disagree. This action in submission to the guidance of the Holy Spirit usually brings peace. However, in some cases we promote conflict resolution by pulling the people together.

This drawing people together can be done informally. Suppose some church members are arguing about what kinds of music are appropriate for the main church service. One group wants older hymns, and the other wants modern music such as Scripture choruses. One strategy is to gather all the concerned members and let them work out a solution.

Or the meeting may be formal. Imagine a church dispute so complex that it is difficult even to describe it—yet this really happened. Brother Bob introduces Brother Jim and other members to Mr. Smith, a nonmember, who is raising money to start a business. Brother Jim and others lend Mr. Smith some money. But he runs off with it, and they never see Mr. Smith again.

Brother Jim and others claim that back when they were making the loans, Brother Bob said he would stand behind them. They feel that Bob should repay them the money they lost. Brother Bob denies securing the loans. The arguing and hard feelings are tearing apart the church.

Many of the members think the church should ignore the war. They say, "The church is for its members' spiritual development—not solving all their problems." Time does not heal this wound. Every day it looks more and more as if someone will sue.

Finally the minister, with the blessing of the board, gets all the parties to agree to binding arbitration. Three respected denominational lawyers are brought in, and the parties meet and explain their positions. The pastor instructs the lawyers to decide the issue, using both the technical legal applications and the principle of fairness. That is, the law may require signed papers that guarantee the loan, but this should not be a loophole that lets Brother Bob off the hook if he made pledges about the loan.

The binding arbitration agreement includes a provision that stops the parties from talking about the conflict with other members. The minister moderates the proceeding and, according to the agreement, invites the entire congregation to attend.

The process proves highly successful. Everyone agrees that the settlement is fair. The parties are spared high legal costs. They preserve a moderate degree of church unity, and amazingly, the minister emerges as the great peacemaker.

Governance Meetings

The last type of committee is governance. Earlier we compared churches and businesses, pointing out that some ministers see themselves as entrepreneurs who pull together the various elements that are needed to get a job done. We must not carry this analogy too far, because we can also compare churches and governments.

A church is a group working together for common purposes, interests, and standards. The only church meetings recorded in the Bible were for governing church standards, as in Acts 15. Governance meetings are the church's legislative process. The focus is on seeking God's will for his people in church discipline, church goals, membership policy, ordination policy, and so forth.

The real work involved in a legislative type of meeting takes place beforehand. Someone identifies problems and drafts a solution. Then the legislative group amends the proposal as needed and ratifies the solution.

Here the model of majority rule makes more sense than in the other types of meetings. Nevertheless, the ultimate goal is not "What do most people want?" but rather "What is God's will for his church?"

Because the group is acting on recommendations and not problem solving, it can be larger than other kinds of groups. But it should be small enough that members feel responsible for their actions. And because it involves governance, it should be representative.

COMMITTEE SIZE

Choosing the right committee size and makeup is a combination of art and science. Many factors must be balanced.

1. *The more complex the decision, the smaller and more specialized the group must be.* For example, a group for setting up the church's retirement program will be smaller and more specialized than a group working on the missions program.

Another small, specialized type of committees might be a committee that selects music for the main service—a small committee that should have members who are gifted and knowledgeable in music and worship. A committee that plans a church banquet should be small and have people who know how to organize such an event.

2. *The wider the committee's impact, the larger and more democratic it should be.* A committee that chooses the sanctuary carpeting should have a broad range of members selected from the church's subgroups. This provides diverse input and encourages a large support base for fund-raising.

3. *The more the activity depends on volunteer help, the larger the group.* The principle here is that the people who do the work should make the decisions. Conversely, the people who are not doing the work should not make the decisions.

4. *The more governance the group exercises, the larger*

the group. A large group can better represent the congregation's different interests.

5. *The smaller the group, the better.* There are several reasons for keeping groups as small as possible for the task. Small groups will often make better decisions and make them more quickly than larger groups. Members of small groups will feel responsible for their decisions. They are more careful thinkers and will work harder to follow up on their decisions and make them work.

Think about committees on which you have served. If you were one of several score, you put less thought into the decision making than if you were one in a dozen. This is because you feel less influential in the large group, so why work to develop and debate a position? Also, if the group is large, you will feel little shame if the group's decision proves wrong. Moreover, you would not feel a great sense of responsibility to follow through and make the decision work. With small groups, the opposite holds true.

Weigh the size factor of each group when determining the group's composition. Some factors may work at cross purposes, so you need the right balance for size, representation, and expertise. Skillfully balance all the factors as you develop the right group for the job.

Chapter 4

Before the Meeting

It is a cold, cold morning. Brother Brian is in the bow of the boat. Brother Brian is a puzzle to Pastor Jim. He has been a church member for years. He gives and attends faithfully. He is also a church board member, but he never speaks at meetings—not a word. Once Pastor Jim called on Brian for the opening prayer. Brian prayed gracefully, but later asked Jim not to call on him again. The casual onlooker might regard Brian as mentally slow, yet his business success is amazing. He started and manages a firm that manufactures computer disk drives. He was twice elected the entrepreneur of the year in his state, and several business magazines have featured him. Yet Brian remains a puzzle.

To Pastor Jim, Brian seems to be a faithful Christian, but Brian's wife never attends church with him. His grown children often visit the church with him on holidays.

Before the Meeting

After a service Brian is cordial to Pastor Jim on the way out of the church: "Thank you for the sermon, Pastor." Brian does not talk with other members. There has never been such a faithful member whom Pastor Jim knows so little about. Jim has never felt as if he has really ministered to Brian.

Then two days ago Brian telephoned with an invitation. "Jim, this is Brian White. Would you like to shoot at some ducks Thursday morning?"

Jim responded reflexively, "Sure!"

"Great! I'll pick you up at five o'clock."

Afterward Jim mused, "Finally, a chance to get to know Brian." Then it hit him: "I don't know anything about duck hunting. I don't own a gun. I don't own any funny-looking duck-hunting clothes. Didn't I give a talk against hunting in my college ethics class? What am I doing?"

He called Brian back. "Brian, thanks for the invitation, but I don't know anything about hunting. I don't have a gun, and I don't have any duck-hunting clothes."

"Don't worry. I'll bring a gun for you. Just dress warmly. No one will see you except the lady at the diner when we stop for coffee. Oh yeah! Don't worry about *killing* the ducks. See you Thursday."

Thursday morning comes. It is cold. At the boat landing Brian sets up a few tin cans on a log and explains how to shoot the gun.

"The most important thing is not to shoot me. The next important thing is not to shoot yourself. Shooting someone else makes you feel worse than shooting yourself.

"Now, release the safety. Look through the scope. Line up the target in the cross hairs, and squeeze the trigger."

Jim takes a few shots and finally hits a can. Brian says, "Good! Now, when you see the ducks, get them in your sight and then aim just a few feet behind them."

"A few feet behind them? I thought you aimed a few feet before them."

"You do if you want to kill them. I just assumed you wouldn't want to kill them. I always aim a few feet behind them so I don't accidentally hit them."

Jim smiles. "How long have you been doing this?"

"Since I was a little boy. My daddy took me duck hunting. I loved spending time with him. I loved the early morning and the frost. But I hated killing ducks. My daddy told me just to aim a few feet behind them so I would miss them. And that is what I do."

The two men climb into the boat and start out. As they are waiting in the blind, Brian says, "Brother Ebenezer is giving you quite a time in the board meetings."

"Yeah, sometimes I feel like chucking it in. He can be hardheaded."

"Don't sweat it. He likes you better than any minister we've ever had."

"Well, sometimes I feel like a fool at the board meetings. I wish I knew what I was doing wrong."

Brian hesitates. "I'll tell you if you really want me to." Jim nods.

"You run a good meeting. You are fair and honest and you listen to us when we talk." (A strange comment, Jim thinks, since Brian never talks). "What you do wrong is not prepare for the meeting. Running my company is one meeting after another. I run about half of them, and I spend hours getting ready for them. The agenda is more than just listing things to cover. Sometimes I feel that you come into a meeting without thinking about what we must cover.

"But I don't want to sit out here and tell you everything you need to do. I saw a book in the Christian bookstore called *Making Comittees Work* by Mack Tennyson. It might help. It is not a great book, but it does have a good hunting story in it."

About that time some ducks fly over. Jim aims and fires. The ducks fly on. Brian aims and fires. The ducks fly on.

Brian says, "Man! You call us hunters! They flew right by and we still missed them. Well, we'll do better next time."

PURPOSE

The most important thing about running a meeting does not happen at the meeting. It happens beforehand. Preparing is the best thing we can do to ensure having a successful meeting. The first step is to state the meeting's purpose.

Many meetings start with the time-worn phrase, "We all know why we are here." Most people attending a meeting do *not* know why they are there. Until a few minutes before the meeting, it was just a calendar entry. To state the meeting's purpose at the beginning is important. Devising the purpose is more difficult than we may think.

When we state the meeting's purpose, we must be sure to do it right: (1) a well-stated purpose is focused on the outcome, (2) it is expressed in a way whereby we can measure success, and (3) it is realistic.

Consider this poorly worded purpose: "There is a youth directors' meeting next Monday night. We will meet to discuss the youth program." It does not have a focus for the group on any particular task or situation, so when the meeting is over, how do we guage whether the meeting was a success?

Here is a properly worded purpose: "There is a youth directors' meeting next Monday night. We will prepare next year's youth event schedule." This clearly stated purpose sets the meeting's tone. It is the anchor that keeps the group focused on a task.

With the poorly stated purpose, the discussion can lead almost anywhere. The properly stated purpose limits the topic to scheduling. The poorly stated purpose gives no basis for reviewing how well the meeting fulfills its goal. The properly stated purpose gives a concrete basis: How much of the schedule was completed? So the first planning step is clearly to state the meeting's purpose.

CAN THIS MEETING BE AVOIDED?

After stating the objective, decide whether you really need this meeting. Is the purpose of a nature—such as a specific action—that is better handled by an individual decision maker? If so, why not let one person make the decision? Or does the purpose have a focus on policy and therefore belong to a group?

Can the purpose wait until another meeting, when

41

several topics can be combined? Is the purpose only advising another group? We should do away with groups that merely advise groups higher up. Either let the final decision rest with the lower group, or let the upper group make the decision. Always consider the option of not having the meeting.

REVIEWING THE GROUP

You have decided that the meeting is necessary. The next step is to review the group who will meet to carry out the stated purpose. Is this the right group? Does it have the power to fulfill the purpose? If an action-type decision is called for, is this group the one to carry it out? If this will be a legislative-type decision, is the group sufficiently representative? Decide whether you have the right group to fulfill the meeting's purpose. If you do not, change groups.

THE MEETING PLACE

Now it is time to select a meeting place. The purpose and type of meeting determine the site. The meeting could be held either at the church or elsewhere, even if it involves church business.

At the Church

Meeting in the church facility has some advantages. It is convenient and familiar to most members. Church resources are available during the meeting—photocopier, clerical help, and materials are all readily available. Convening elsewhere may entail a cost for the meeting room.

Nevertheless, there are some disadvantages in meeting at the church. There may be workaday noise and interruptions such as telephone calls. Also, people may be less likely to take a fresh look at a problem when they are meeting in the same old place. Finally, meeting in the church building can weaken the task of building the group's commitment to a problem.

If we decide to meet at the church, we must think creatively. Meet in the kitchen and eat watermelon. Sit on the back steps and get some fresh air. Sit in the location pertinent to the topic on the agenda. That is, for planning music, sit in the choir loft. If you are working on a youth program, sit in their classrooms. Think creatively.

Nonchurch Locations

The good reasons to meet at the church are the poor reasons to meet elsewhere, and vice versa. There are some good reasons for meeting away from the church. People may treat a meeting as more important when it is held at a special place. Meet somewhere offsite if it is a new group and you need to build a sense of teamwork; such a location contributes to collegiality and a team spirit.

Perhaps a succession of meetings on a difficult topic is wearing out the group members. Meet at a new location to inject life into these meetings. If the building committee is meeting every Thursday night, change the location occasionally.

Be creative in choosing a nonchurch location. Use a meeting room at a nearby restaurant or hotel. Go to the country club. Use the town hall or the public meeting room of a bank.

Meeting in a Home

If you meet in someone's home, problems may arise such as the ringing of the phone or disturbance by children. Also, the meeting burdens the host in preparing the home, and etiquette usually demands the offer of something to eat.

But there are advantages that commend a home for meetings. If a small church is without comfortable meeting rooms, a home may be an inexpensive option. Also, as with other nonchurch sites, meeting in a home helps to build collegiality and team spirit. Don't overlook the possibility that meeting in someone's home will bring out a civility that may not be present in a less casual setting like a meeting room.

Preparing the Meeting Room

No matter where a meeting is to be held, good leaders will ensure that the room conditions are favorable. Arrange the tables to seat everyone comfortably. Make sure the lighting and the air conditioning or heat are properly set. Provide for abundant drinking water. Add a special touch that shows you care about the members, such as an exotic refreshment or a flower for each table or person.

THE AGENDA

An agenda is crucial to a meeting's success. It puts the meeting's purpose in focus and sets the tone for the task at hand. It is also the best tool for controlling the meeting's progress. There are two ways to approach agendas.

The Classic Agenda

The classic agenda is essentially a work list. It sets out the meeting's events in this way:

1. Call to order
2. Opening exercises (e.g., devotions)
3. Roll call
4. Reading and approval of minutes
5. Reports of official boards and standing committees
6. Reports of special committees
7. Special orders
8. Unfinished business
9. New business
10. Good of the order
11. Announcements
12. Adjournment

This approach has advantages. It follows the fair rule: the first business in is the first business out. So with time all items get covered. The approach also has the advantage that people are used to seeing work arranged this way. But there are some drawbacks that may be remedied in a more thoughtful approach.

Before the Meeting

A More Thoughtful Agenda

Classic agendas organizes a meeting's tasks. The thoughtful agenda organizes the time. Meetings are planned around the way groups make decisions. Here is a basic outline:

1. Opening exercises
2. Minutes
3. Announcements
4. Easy items
5. Moderate items
6. Difficult items
7. Discussion-only items
8. Easiest item
9. Closing and adjournment

Opening exercises. A typical church meeting opens and closes with prayer as a matter of form. It is the meeting's most important part, as you already know.

Minutes. Minutes record the decisions and main ideas for or against the actions of the previous meeting. They do not report all the discussion. The agenda must give members an opportunity to review and approve the previous meeting's minutes. This item is often treated as trivial, but it is important, because it gives the group a chance to reunify and reestablish the momentum that was formed at the earlier meeting.

[*Reports.*] A typical meeting has reports from different people representing, for example, subcommittees or departments. The best way to handle the report section is to eliminate it. Reports are great time-wasters and add little to a meeting's success. It is tiring to sit through endless reports that may not look at vital issues.

If upon consideration you decide that you must have reports, organize them well. Before placing a report on the agenda, talk to the presenter. Discern the major issues, and seek a way to focus the group on the issues without wasting time. Settle on a time limit for the report and hold the presenter to it.

Announcements. A time for announcements relates to routine business. If the agenda is not long, allow any group member to make an announcement, even if it is irrelevant to the meeting's purpose. Affirm the members for the committee work they have done or for personal successes. Open announcements build collegiality and motivation.

Decision items. Place easier items before more difficult ones on the agenda. (But hold off on the easiest one, for reasons to be explained below.) This builds a group's momentum for making decisions. Without this momentum, it is easy to get bogged down, and the group will waste its time on the first agenda item.

Discussion-only items. Include a section in the agenda for items that need discussion but not an immediate decision. These are usually matters that ultimately need a decision, but final action can take place at a later meeting. This strategy has several advantages.

First, it allows feelings to be aired without running the risk of hastily made decisions. Suppose the youth minister took the young people someplace that was not viewed favorably. Everyone thinks the youth minister needs some censure for this error in judgment. Designating this a discussion-only item in the agenda allows the board members to express feelings without pressure to take action that they may regret later as too extreme.

Second, with discussion-only items, church leaders can view the group's direction without taking a specific position. Suppose the senior pastor thinks the youth minister should be fired, but the board members consider a strong warning more appropriate. If the matter is dealt with as a discussion-only item, the senior pastor can search out the group's thinking without advancing a certain position.

Third, discussion-only items allow time for working out

compromises between meetings. Suppose Brother Ebenezer is the only board member who wants the youth minister fired. During the discussion-only time Ebenezer can clearly and forcefully state his views. Knowing what we do about human nature, it is unfair to expect Brother Ebenezer to change his position quickly after he has so eloquently stated it. If there is time between the discussion and the final decision, members can work out a face-saving compromise.

Fourth, discussion-only items give members more thinking time and praying time before deciding on the right action.

Fifth, because the item is for discussion only, it is easier to manage the time spent on the matter. A group will usually carry on a discussion until they reach a decision, no matter how long that takes. The situation is open-ended, and if they make no decision the group will feel they have wasted their time. But with discussion-only items, the chair can end the discussion properly. This is painless, because there will be time at the next meeting for further discussion as needed.

Sixth, because the item is for discussion only, it is easier to keep the group working on the higher general principles they want instead of focusing on details. This prevents the seesaw effect seen in typical group decision making, in which the group goes from discussing general principles to specific details and back to general principles and so forth. This becomes very tiring. Discussion-only time can keep members focused on the general principles, allowing the opportunity to work out the specific details later.

A tool that can facilitate discussion-only items is the straw vote. Straw votes are nonbinding votes that test the group's feelings. They enable the church leaders to develop a final action based on the group's sentiments.

Remember the youth leader who was in trouble? Suppose the board members take a straw vote to send him a letter of censure. On the basis of that straw vote, the leadership has a chance to draft a letter and explore the feelings of the congregation unofficially on the matter.

Easiest item. Often a group has easy items to decide. Save one easy item for last. This ends the meeting on a positive note. Note the flow of the agenda, beginning with easy items to build momentum, going to difficult items, and concluding with an easy item for a positive adjournment.

Closing and adjournment. Closing prayer is the most important item on the agenda.

TIMING

Time is an important factor in managing an agenda. Agendas help to budget the time frames in a meeting. Usually people make agendas without thinking about time. If the meeting is to last two hours, however, then set an agenda that can be fulfilled in two hours. Overloading a meeting frustrates the members and causes them to hurry through decision making. It takes away the feelings of accomplishment members should have when a meeting is over.

Make meetings last less than three hours, unless there is a major break. Divide the meeting time into thirds. Spend the first third on the opening prayer, announcements, and easy decision items. Spend the second third on more difficult decision items. Then spend the last third on the discussion-only items, easiest items, and closing prayer.

Why should we divide the time this way? During the first third the meeting is gaining momentum. Members may arrive late. The group reestablishes bonding. The focus on decision making is growing. Handling the easier items fosters this process.

During the middle third the members are at their mental and physical peak. They are fresh and have already enjoyed making a few decisions. Their attention span is the longest. At this time the attendance is best, because the latecomers and the early leavers are all present. The momentum for decision making is at its highest. So the group is ready to handle difficult decisions.

The final third sees people tired and anxious to leave.

The decision-making momentum is waning. It is the best time for the discussion-only items.

The One-Hour Law

No agenda item should take more than one hour. Time the discussion. If fifty minutes have passed, take inventory. Perhaps the group cannot make a decision. Perhaps essential information is missing. The decision may be too complex for the meeting situation.

If the group does not make a decision within fifty minutes, the chair should declare, "Something is wrong. Why have we not been able to make a decision? Let's talk about why we haven't made a decision." Limit the discussion to that. By the hour's end the group will have developed a way to deal with the problem of decision making. The solution may be simply to table the matter until more thought can be given to it. Perhaps dividing the problem into smaller, more manageable parts is the key. A subcommittee may need to work out the details to make the decision clearer for the larger group. The subcommittee can break down the issue to examine its various parts; it should not spend more than an hour on each component. No issue should require more than an hour of a committee's time.

Time Budgets

Try putting a time budget on the agenda. A time budget is an estimate of how long a particular matter of business should take. This budget should not be used to stifle a full discussion; rather, you should use it to guide discussion and keep the meeting moving.

Chapter 5

To Chair or Not to Chair a Committee

What a peaceful Saturday night! It is Pastor Jim's first night off in weeks. "I'll stay home and relax. That's all. Maybe I'll watch a little TV. Maybe I'll build a fire and get cozy with Mrs. Pastor Jim. Who knows? Nights off are great."

There is a hitch: Pastor Jim's fifteen-year-old daughter and Tina, her "spend-the-night" friend. Another problem looms: a sixteen-year-old boy. Pastor Jim has seen him around. He thinks the kid is okay, but who really knows about sixteen-years-olds? The three teenagers are visiting in the den, which has the fireplace and the television set.

Jim is sitting in the kitchen reading yesterday's paper and eating ice cream. His daughter walks in and asks, "Can we go downtown for some ice cream?"

Pastor Jim could not resist saying, "What's wrong with the ice cream we have here?"

50

"Daddy!"

"Well, I really don't feel like driving you downtown."

"Ted'll drive us."

"Ted? That little boy?"

"Please, Daddy, he is such a safe driver. And we will be back by ten. Please, Daddy."

"Okay, but I want you and Tina home at ten and I want Ted gone."

Pastor Jim gives up on the idea of building a fire. Maybe a smooch during a "Golden Girls" commercial will do. Then at nine Tina's parents call to ask her some question. Pastor Jim explains, "I let them go get ice cream downtown with Ted." Something else is said, and Jim responds, "He seems like a good kid. They are to be home by ten." Jim hangs up the phone and has a brief anxiety attack. Then he settles down to snooze before the television—a hobby that meetings and visitation usually prevent.

At ten the phone rings and Jim figures it is his daughter calling to beg for more time. But it is Tina's parents. It seems that Tina can go out only with her parents' approval, even when she is staying at someone else's home. They are coming to get her. This would not bother Jim so much, except the kids are not home yet, and he realizes he forgot Ted's last name. He prays.

It is a race between the teenagers and Tina's father. Will they reach Jim's house before the father? The kids lose, and Jim must make embarrassing small talk, hoping that Tina's father does not ask Ted's last name. Finally Ted drops the girls off. Tina and her father leave. Pastor Jim dutifully scolds his daughter, and everyone goes to bed, but not to sleep.

LEADING MEETINGS

How do the problems of teenage children relate to leading meetings? There are many parallels. The parents want teenagers to develop, be free, be successful, and enjoy their friends. However, parents must also show leadership, control, and authority. The good parent balances all these qualities. The good meeting leader does the same.

The good meeting leader wants the members to be creative, develop personally, be free to express creative ideas, and enjoy one another's company. The group also needs leadership, control, and authority to evoke these feelings.

With teenagers, too much freedom destroys the things they want. Teenagers who are addicted to drugs have no freedom, are unable to enjoy friends, and short-circuit personal growth. Likewise, committees with too much freedom destroy the very qualities the members want. To balance all this is the task of a parent on the one hand and a committee leader on the other.

If we want a committee to be creative and fully developed, our leadership must be transparent. The members must not think we are forcing them to move in a certain direction. Our job is to balance the forces that lead to creative decisions. Our influence ends there.

JOB DESCRIPTION: THE SERVANT-LEADER

The chair is a servant-leader, the committee's servant. If we define our leadership as servanthood, it is more fun. You may ask, What fun is it to lead a group through a decision on what color to paint the sanctuary? Yet, serving the group in personal spiritual growth is fun. The sanctuary color is a minor issue.

Christ's life supports the servant-leader model. "Jesus called the Twelve and said, 'If anyone wants to be first, he must be the very last, and the servant of all' " (Mark 9:35). In servanthood we place our temporal wants after others' spiritual needs. All great people (and chairpeople) do this.

A servant-leader fulfills four functions: meeting leader, administrator, spokesperson, and head.

The Servant-Leader as Leader

The chair is the group's leader. This involves more than just running the meeting. The chairperson must manage the entire process of defining the group's purpose, selecting goals, defining decision alternatives, and seeing that the decision is carried out.

To Chair or Not to Chair a Committee

The chairperson is the group's main visionary. He or she has the clearest idea about where the group goes next. This holds risks for the leader, because the leader's focus is to be on process, not on outcome. Suppose a church forms a committee to change its system of government. The current bylaws place governance in the hands of a few men, but the congregation believes that the times dictate a broader, more diverse style of governance.

The chair has a clear idea about what he or she thinks is the best solution: a strong church board comprising so many men and so many women elected from the membership. But the chair must set aside personal ideas about the outcome in order to focus on the process. First, the group must decide how decisions of the church should be made. Does it want power centered in one board or spread over many? Then it must decide what groups report to which board. And finally it must decide what type of person is in each group.

The next task for the chair is to refine and divide these steps into substeps. These are the steps that it appears the committee must go through in deciding between dispersed power or concentrated power: (1) Read the articles on church governance supporting each view, (2) assign members to interview members from other churches who have tried either model, (3) then list the pros and cons related to each choice. Again, the chair's focus is on process, not outcome.

Good leaders must juggle two interests that have the potential to harmonize or to conflict. First, they must focus on people. How do they draw out the best from the committee members? Second, they focus on ideas. How can they nurture the birth and development of ideas? The people focus and the idea focus are equally important. Good leaders can foster a mentally safe environment that encourages people to express ideas freely and then nurture the ideas toward a final decision. Here—with a decision—the two focuses come into harmony.

We can focus on ideas and ignore the committee members' feelings so much that they will stop introducing and nurturing ideas. This happens when there is great pressure to make decisions prematurely or when a leader pushes one idea so strongly that the members feel intimidated and hesitant to offer another.

Conversely, we can focus too much on people. We can be so concerned about people's feelings and their mental state that the group never gets around to making a decision. Everyone is happy, but no one is working.

The goal is to balance the responsibilities of nurturing ideas and nurturing people. This is the group leader's job.

The Servant-Leader as Director

The committee chair sees to it that someone does what has to be done. The chair's duties include scheduling meeting rooms, sending agendas, copying handouts, and seeing that the minutes are sent out. The list goes on and on. Many items are trivial, but many set the tone for an entire meeting. If we want a report from the building subcommittee, we must make sure that someone from that group is present and prepared. Calling on someone for a report without warning is unfair and disrupts the progress of the meeting.

Many chairpersons fail because they neglect the many mundane tasks in favor of more visible ones. A chair may accept the job for the sake of leading a meeting without thinking about all the hidden duties. People sometimes choose chairs who have the skill to bring out the best in people. We often see this trait in people who do not work well with details. If you fall into this group, develop for yourself a manager's checklist to work through routinely for each meeting (see chart).

The Servant-Leader as Spokesperson

The role of spokesperson can be both enjoyable and risky. The chair is the person who tells the world of the group's decisions. It is enjoyable being the one who gives the information, but it is risky because it is easy to embarrass yourself by doing it wrong. Suppose the building committee decides to sell some property. If enough money is raised, the committee will look at building a gymnasium. The chair

MANAGER'S CHECKLIST

Task	Person Asked		Followup
	Name	Date	Date

Task	Person Asked Name	Date	Followup Date
Time set	_____	____	____
Room scheduled	_____	____	____
Agenda prepared	_____	____	____
Special participants notified[1]	_____	____	____
	_____	____	____
	_____	____	____
	_____	____	____
Meeting announce-ment sent	_____	____	____
Refreshments	_____	____	____
Room prepared	_____	____	____
Handouts prepared	_____	____	____
Minutes sent	_____	____	____
Decisions sent[2]	_____	____	____
Thank-you notes sent	_____	____	____
Meeting evaluation done	_____	____	____

[1] These are people who are needed to make the meeting work, either with special reports or special expertise.
[2] This is the step at which the chair sends the committee's final decision to the proper authority (e.g., a parent committee or the pastor).

reports to the church board, "We are selling the property and building a gym." This proves to be an embarrassment when enough money is in hand but the building committee decides to do something else with it.

The servant-leader should be very careful about keeping his personal remarks out of the reporting.

The Servant-Leader as Meeting Head

The role of meeting head is what we most commonly think of as regards chairs. In this role the servant-leader leads the meetings and has three major functions. First, he must provide orderly procedures. That is, the chair is the "fairness sheriff." Fairness requires that each member be equal: Each has an equal chance to speak, an equal responsibility to contribute, and an equal say in the final decision. Fairness also demands that issues be treated impartially. Impartiality is different from equality. Important things receive more time; unimportant things, less time. Using Roberts Rules of Order is one way to achieve fairness (see chapter 10).

Second, the meeting leader has to guide the group's decision making. A group without a leader never makes decisions. When assigned leaders fail to lead the group to a decision, someone else emerges as an informal leader and fulfills the role. Until then the group just spins its wheels.

Here is a good way to shepherd the group toward a decision. Let the members talk about the issue for perhaps ten minutes. If one theme emerges, interject, "I think I hear us heading toward such-and-such a decision." If it seems that there is consensus on that score, then lead the group to fill in the details. If several people oppose the idea, then allow further discussion until you get another vision of the way the group is going. Then say, "So now I hear us heading toward such-and-such a decision." Keep working this way until you nudge the group to a firm decision.

The guidance process is not always focused on the final decision. It can simply help the group formulate intermediate decisions. Suppose the committee is choosing a new color scheme for the sanctuary. The chair opens the floor for discussion. Many people talk, and after a while the chair senses that most people prefer a pastel shade. The chair suggests, "So I think we are agreeing on a pastel shade?" This helps the group narrow down the decision. Most committee decisions really combine many smaller decisions.

The third servant-leader role is the position of authority. That is, the leader can use authority in defending other members' rights, in sanctioning members who are out of line, or in prodding the group to work toward a decision.

This authority is implicit in chairing a committee, and members expect you to use it. And they expect you to use it kindly.

Here again we encounter a balancing act. A chair who relies on authority instead of leadership is remiss. The chair may exercise authority heavy-handedly in saying, "We only have a few minutes to work on this agenda item, so we need to make a decision." By contrast, using more subtle leadership skills to accomplish the same goal is better.

SELF-EVALUATION

Do you ever wonder whether the apostle Paul intended to draw funny pictures in his letters? Some word pictures in his Corinthians letter are really quite humorous.

> And if the ear should say, "Because I am not an eye, I do not belong to the body," it would not for that reason cease to be part of the body. If the whole body were an eye, where would the sense of hearing be? If the whole body were an ear, where would the sense of smell be? But in fact God has arranged the parts in the body, every one of them, just as he wanted them to be (1 Cor. 12:16–18).

> And in the church God has appointed first of all apostles, second prophets, . . . those with gifts of administration . . ." (1 Cor. 12:28).

It is unreasonable to think that God gives one person the gifts needed for every sphere of church leadership. It is rare to find a person gifted in public speaking, visiting, ministering to the sick, relating with young people, church administration, and so forth. Every church leader must assess his or her gifts and use wisdom in finding the proper role.

These concepts are not only sound theologically, but also effective practically: (1) Ministers are not always the right people for chairing committees, and (2) good committee members do not always grow into good chairs.

SHOULD I CHAIR THIS GROUP?

There are three parts to the question of whether one of us should chair a committee: (1) Should I chair anything? (2) Should I chair this committee? (3) Should I chair this meeting?

It is consistent with the apostle Paul's discussion of gifts that many church leaders should never chair meetings. Their gifts lie elsewhere. How do you stack up according to the job description given earlier in this chapter? Do you like handling details? How well do you lead small groups? Are you adept at gently keeping people on track? Do you like reserving your own ideas and helping others to express theirs? If your answer to any of these questions is no, then it is better that someone else chair the committee. According to Paul's discussion of gifts, your church has someone gifted in chairing committees.

You may believe you are gifted in chairing committees and yet recognize that there are certain committees you should not chair. To conduct a meeting properly takes time. It is common for ministers to chair all or most of the church committees. This is bad for the minister, and it is bad for the membership. The minister is very likely to do a poor job because of overcommitment of time, and the members are not able to develop gifts of church leadership. Many ministers enlist members to chair less important meetings while they retain control of those they consider the most important. This is not the best way to help the church. This approach suggests, "I trust you with the church music committee, but I can't trust you with the church board."

Do not try to chair all the important committees. Is your purpose for being on a committee to minister to the members? You can do that in any type of meeting, not just the important ones. Ministering to the church music committee should be just as fulfilling as ministering to the church board.

Another reason not to chair a committee is that its purpose may be contrary to what you want. You may want the congregation to build a new church, but the board prefers to remodel the existing building. You may not be the most appropriate person to chair the remodeling committee.

"Should I chair this meeting?" You feel strongly about a topic at a certain meeting. You know what the church needs, and you want to work to achieve it. Enlist someone else to chair that meeting; then you are free from the neutral stance that is required of chairs. Simply say, "I have strong feeling about today's agenda item. So Brother Fred will chair today's meeting." People respect your giving up power to avoid abusing it.

There is an unexpected drawback to not chairing committees. Although members want the chair to be neutral on issues, people expect members to align themselves on one side or another. It might be better for a minister to chair the committee and work hard not to align with either side. On controversial issues it is good to have one person not aligned with any faction. Chairing the committee may be the only way to keep out of the fray.

Being a regular committee member instead of a chairperson improves rapport between the pastor and church members. This important benefit prompts many pastors to give up the gavel for good.

Chapter 6

The Best Committee Members

It was the Mother of All Meetings. That is the way heaven's annals on Shulerville Community Church may record the meeting. The meeting was about firing Pastor Jim. This was not a meeting hastily called at the instigation of some angry, bellyaching church member. The charges against Jim were serious, and even you may feel that there were sufficient grounds for firing him.[1]

It happened this way. Brother Brock collects and sells aluminum cans. He feels it is a good way to spend time, because it helps the environment and gives him exercise. One day he was checking for cans along Highway 341 when he saw Pastor Jim's car partially hidden in the woods.

---

[1]I hope they don't fire Pastor Jim, because I need his help to finish the book.

Halfway curious and halfway concerned for Jim, Brother Brock went to look. As he neared the spot, he could see Jim sitting in the car and smoking marijuana—he could smell the telltale odor. Brother Brock quietly backed away and began walking toward Shulerville on Highway 341. Pastor Jim passed him on his way to town.

After three restless nights, Brother Brock decided he must confide in someone. He talked to Brother Garvin. Brother Brock thought he could trust him, but he was wrong. Before long the whole church knew, and that led to this meeting, called to discuss what to do about Pastor Jim.

Brother Don chaired the meeting, which began with heartfelt prayer. Jim was called on to defend himself. Jim declared, "I know this is very serious, and I know that self-justification is wrong. But let me explain. It is not as serious as you think. You all know that I often used drugs in my younger days before I became a Christian. Last Thursday—that was two days before Brother Brock saw me—I saw a cellophane bag with the stuff" (he could not bring himself to say "marijuana") "in the church dumpster. I was taking out the garbage, and there it was lying on top. I promise that this has not been a regular problem with me. Well, I just ignored it and went back into my study. Then I thought about it more and more. I decided that it wasn't safe just lying out there— you know how the church kids play around the dumpster. So I brought it into the office until I could call the police."

Brother Ebenezer shook his head in disbelief.

"It stayed in the office for a day," Pastor Jim continued. "All the time I sat there thinking about it. Finally I decided to smoke it for old time's sake. So I drove out of town, and that is where Brother Brock saw me. I promise this is not a regular problem with me."

Some members responded with sympathetic murmurs. Others gave murmurs of disbelief. But everyone murmured. A few asked Pastor Jim questions, and after that he left. And then things really started. One could imagine a host of unseen angels hovering in the room out of curiosity.

Brother Ebenezer fired the first volley. "We must fire him. He confessed to the whole thing just now."

Brother Brock said, "I don't think so. I believe him. Firing him would destroy the best minister I know."

Sister Sarah said, "I always heard that if you use that stuff just once, it hooks you for life."

Brother John said, "No, that is crack cocaine. Marijuana just makes you crazy. I once heard about a man who used it. He flew off a building—thought he was a bird or something."

Brother Ebenezer said, "You don't know what you are talking about."

"You don't have to get so upset."

"I'm not upset! You just don't know what you are talking about. That is not the issue. The issue is about keeping a pastor who shows such poor judgment."

The unseen angels leaned forward with greater interest.

"I once used marijuana. It's no big deal."

"Illegal drugs are still illegal drugs."

"We must uphold church standards. What will people say when they discover we have a minister that uses drugs?"

"What'll people say when they discover we are forgiving?"

Some of the angels cocked their heads to hear better.

The debate raged for several hours. Finally the members voted, and the outcome was thirteen to two in favor of keeping Jim. Everyone knew that Brother Ebenezer had cast one of the two negative votes—the church wondered for weeks who cast the other one.

The meeting adjourned, and the angels went on about their duties fully satisfied.

After church the next Sunday the most amazing thing happened. All the members were lingering on the lawn after leaving the main service. Pastor Jim was at the door shaking hands. Some people were a little nervous about approaching Jim, but everyone wanted to.

Out on the lawn a church member asked Brother Ebenezer what happened at the meeting. Brother Ebenezer said, "We discussed it and voted to keep him."

That was all he said, and that is amazing. Brother Ebenezer must be a better person than you thought.

THE COMMITTEE MEMBER'S JOB

Before we accept a seat on a committee, we must be sure we understand our duties and the commitment we are making. Each committee is different on these matters. After we understand our duties and commitment, we should evaluate them in terms of our personal agendas and ascertain that there is no conflict.

Ponder these questions: Do you have the time to serve this group? Do you have sympathy for the committee's purpose? Do your personal beliefs conflict with the purpose? Can you work with the chair? Answering "no" suggests you must have some compelling reason to serve on the committee—perhaps a strong commitment to a cause. If you cannot work well with the chair, but the project excites you, perhaps you should take the job. If you are very busy and committed to other things, but like working with the chair, you may want to reorder your priorities and serve on the committee.

Personal Beliefs

The questions about personal belief structure need a closer look. In general you want to have some sympathy for the committee's purpose. If a committee is selecting a piano and you oppose buying a piano, then you should not serve on the committee. However, do not take this too far. A study committee that is looking at whether the congregation should build a new church needs some members who oppose the idea. The dissenting members inhibit one-sided discussion and make the group more representative of the whole constituency.

Provincialism

Provincialism is a difficult issue. Wider concerns compete against immediate interests where politics or religion is concerned. Should a member of the U.S. Congress fight to keep a military base open in his or her district when the

Pentagon has determined it is no longer needed? Are the legislators to be looking primarily after their districts' affairs, or the country's affairs? These questions are not easily answered.

Eastern Europe and other parts of the world have become newly opened for Christian witness in recent years. Several large denominations are endeavoring to seize the opportunity for evangelism while attending to the congregations back home. Church members from South America vote to accept less money from a denominational missions agency so that more funds will be available for Eastern Europe.

Local church decisions also confront the temptation to provincialism. If you are the youth leader, should you always focus on what is best for the youth, or are there times when you must make a decision that inhibits the youth program, yet benefits the church as a whole? You must balance your group's concerns and the total church needs.

THE SERVANT PREPARING TO MEET

A little homework is needed to prepare for meetings. The first homework assignment is to prepare for the general committee duties. What are the committee's current issues? What background information do you need, and where can you get it? Will your field of expertise be helpful to the committee's fulfilling its purpose? Who is on the committee? Should you meet them beforehand to get a sense of their views?

The second homework assignment is to review the agenda of the next meeting? Read the supporting documents. Perhaps seek clarifying information. Sketch out some alternatives.

The third task is to prepare physically and spiritually. Do you become tired or hungry during a meeting? This is unfair to your group members. Likewise, is your spirit prepared for the meeting? If not, you could completely defeat your purpose for being there. Spend time before the meeting asking God to give wisdom, energy, and a servant attitude. Also, ask God for a chance to minister to a group member's spiritual needs. This service gives meetings a new dimension.

THE SERVANT WORKING AT THE MEETING

At a meeting you juggle three jobs. You are taking the servant role as you serve the meeting's process, content, and people. This book emphasizes that the interpersonal aspects of a committee are more important than the actual content or process. During your committee work attune, like an attentive servant, to opportunities to serve a fellow member's spiritual and emotional needs.

Serving the Process

Good members serve the process by helping the chair lead. This does not mean calling for seconds and votes. Rather, good members help the group move toward decision making. They suggest compromises and options that may work and gain consensus. They use social pressure to restrain troublesome members.

Members are free to express themselves in ways that the chair is not. Suppose a member is talking too much. The chair cannot easily deal with this without appearing autocratic. But a member can readily say, "John, I think we understand you. I want to hear what Mary has to say. I think she knows something about this matter." Many people find it easier to start talking than to stop. They become involved in a speech and find themselves struggling to end it.

There is another special power a member has that the chair does not have. Suppose that the group has become stalled on one agenda item. It has spent too much time on the matter, and the time allowed for the meeting will expire long before the committee has completed the agenda. The chair, however, must be fair and allow each member ample discussion time. By contrast, a member has greater freedom in hurrying the group along: "If we don't hurry, we'll be here 'til midnight." A good member uses this special power to help the progress.

Serving the Content

Members have the servant duty to participate properly. Finding a balance between too much and too little takes wisdom. Too little participation hurts the group. Some people think sitting silently is a virtue, but it can be as disruptive as long-windedness.

People tend to consider a silent person either bored or angry. Concern for the silent member can destroy the decision-making process. If we have not contributed to solving a problem, we can deflect concern by simply giving some approval: "I think this is a good solution."

Although a lack of participation is a concern, most people worry more about their overdoing it. Some people wish more *were* worried about it. I'd like to offer a rule of thumb: The amount of time we speak should be about the same as for everyone else. At some meetings we are free to talk a lot, because everyone else talks a lot. For other meetings, more constraint is appropriate.

Speaking time should average out. If you intend to speak quite a bit on one issue, be more reticent on others that are of less concern to you. Choose one or two items on which you will remain silent. Think of this as each member's having so much participation capital. If the capital is expended on one issue, there is none left for other matters. It is unfortunate if your capital runs out before the committee gets to the item that is really important to you or benefits from your expertise. The servant-member remembers servanthood and moderates his or her participation.

Group members aren't always fair. There are a number of detrimental practices that run counter to the servant-member model. These will be explored in chapter 8, "Games Committees Play," but one warrants attention here. Call it "unspecific criticism": "I just feel really uncomfortable with doing it this way." No further direction or explanation is offered. This tactic forces the group to guess what the problem is. By contrast, all good criticism includes a suggestion, an alternative. One should at least express a specific description of the problem. General fears and anxieties are only destructive.

THE SERVANT WORKING OUTSIDE THE MEETING

Faithful servant-members do more than get their homework done and attend committee meetings. They also gather information and provide analysis that helps the entire group accomplish its goals. These faithful members try to make past decisions work successfully. They meet in subcommittees to work on details for the larger committee. They help the chair plan the agenda or assist in other ways.

THE PROFESSIONAL SERVANT

You can't help but like Brother Ebenezer. He is hardheaded, stubborn, and ultraconservative. Yet you have to admire the way he dealt with the Pastor Jim drug scandal. He had strong reasons for wanting Jim to be fired. He argued his position. No one can accuse Brother Ebenezer of holding back. But we must remember the way he dealt with the issue after the committee voted: He supported the board's decision.

Brother Ebenezer counts it a privilege to serve on the church board and help make decisions that affect the entire church. He realizes that if he undermines the board's decisions he will cause division in the church and impede the spread of the gospel.

True servant-members support a group's decisions even if they voted against them. It is maddening and even unethical when a member sits silently during a discussion and then speaks against it to friends after the meeting. Expulsion from the committee is too good for him. The give-and-take that occurs during a meeting should stay in the meeting.

This does not mean that if we oppose an action we must blindly support the majority view. It means only that we support the group's authority to make the decision and we respect that authority as a willing member of the group. Several simple but honest responses can serve us well in this regard. One response is simply to report the group's action without personal comment. Doing this without bias keeps us honest and sends the implicit message that we are not happy about the action. Another response is to report the arguments for the action from the positive position. "The majority felt that remodeling the old church instead of building a new one saves more money for evangelism."

People who criticize an action are often distancing themselves from it in case events turn out poorly: "Everyone else voted for a new building. I think it is a bad idea because I do not think we have enough money." Or they criticize to build their self-esteem: "The board voted to buy a van. But I think we should save the money. You know what the Bible says about 'a penny saved is a penny earned.' "[2] Most people see these games for what they are and have little respect for the complainer. Undermining a group's decision is the fountainhead of many problems and lost souls.

THE COMMITTED SERVANT

Servant-members are committed to the group and expect others to be committed also. The group's social dynamics always entails some hidden feelings—unspoken feelings that can be very damaging.

Some members may feel that others are not working hard enough. Others resent holding up the meeting to explain details to those who missed the previous meeting. Others resent the resentment they feel from members who expect more than they are giving. A useful tool for dealing with all the uncertainty about commitments is a written "contract" signed by the group members. It covers expectations regarding attendance, confidentiality, expectations about supporting decisions of the group, and other details.

Make the contract's provisions specific: "We will attend ninety percent of the meetings." Not: "We will come to all the meetings we can."

Indicate how discipline will be administered to those

---

[2]Actually Poor Richard said this in his famous almanac, but many people canonize him.

SAMPLE CONTRACT

We the undersigned will attend ninety-five percent of the youth development board's meetings. If we fail, we will buy the members lunch at their favorite restaurant.

We will remain on the board for one year. If we resign before the year is up, we will send each member a handwritten apology and wash the church bus weekly for one month.

We also understand that the meeting's discussions are confidential. Anyone breaking this agreement will resign from the board.

We agree to support the board decisions outside this committee. Anyone breaking this understanding will resign.

We agree to treat each other with Christian courtesy and kindness.

---

who break the agreement. This discipline can take a humorous form: The offender must buy the other members lunch or bring soft drinks to the next meeting. The contract is not legally binding, but it reduces hard feelings and misunderstandings. If we are creative, the contract succeeds in a positive, nonthreatening way.

Chapter 7

After the Meeting

"Don't you see that it is a great thing for us to do?" Pastor Jim was sharing an idea. "I racked my brain for a community-service project for our church, and I think adopting a highway is a great thing. We can get the road that runs right in front of the church."

The church board did not like Pastor Jim's idea. Brother Ebenezer was the most outspoken: "What in tarnation does picking up trash on the highway have to do with spreading the gospel?"

No one asked where "Tar Nation" was. Mostly they wanted to go home.

Jim answered, "It shows that the church is a good citizen and that we can work together. Does everything involve direct evangelism?"

Brother Don said, "Well, if Jim likes picking up trash, I

don't see anything wrong with it. Why don't we let him? I move that we adopt a highway."

Jim felt good as the board unanimously "adopted" the highway according to the program set up by cities for cleaning up roadways. For several weeks Jim ran notices in the church bulletin and newsletter: "Clean up Shulerville. Meet at the church on August 6 for a workbee picking up trash along Johnson Road. It is our civic duty."

Jim talked to several friends. "Do you think this is a good idea—adopting the highway?"

They all said, "Sure! It's a great idea." Truth: If your friends do not have it, who does?

August 6 came. No one showed up. Pastor Jim sat in the church kitchen eating the ice cream he had bought to treat the workers. Plastic bags sat on the counter. The church cat sat eyeing the ice cream.

Jim lamented the vanity. "Why try? What's wrong with adopting a highway? This church is the most unmotivated group. How can I build a fire under them? What am I doing wrong?" These are strange questions to ask a cat.

WHO OWNS THE DECISION?

Shulerville is a motivated church. And adopting a highway is a good idea. The problem lies somewhere else: Pastor Jim did not transfer his ownership of the idea to the group. This is a common error. Obtaining a positive vote does not mean approval, nor does it mean backing. A positive vote only provides a legalistic go-ahead. We must transfer ownership of the idea to the group. This is more difficult to achieve than a positive vote.

Decision ownership means that the members like an idea proposed by someone else as solidly as they like their own ideas. They work to sell it to others as a good plan. They contribute and raise money for it.

Which is a better outcome, owned imperfect plans or perfect plans no one owns? We have seen great ideas fizzle because no one cared about them, and we have seen poor ideas blossom because members got behind them and made them work.

Build ownership in three ways: (1) Through a meeting's content, (2) through post-meeting communication, and (3) through post-meeting duties.

Building Ownership at Meetings

Even before the meeting begins, the chair should look for ways to get the members feeling that they will own forthcoming decisions. One useful way is to distribute all the information concerning a problem before the meeting. Then people arrive already owning solutions. This does hold risks, because there is no difference between your forcing your ideas on the group and someone else's forcing his or hers.

Incubating ideas in a meeting is good for building ownership. There are several ways to do this. Brainstorming is one. Use a flipchart or blackboard. Then specifically state the problem you are working on: "We are looking for some creative senior citizens activities. Give me every idea that comes to mind. Do not worry about how good it sounds; let's just list ideas. There are only two rules: The idea must relate to senior citizens activities, and no one can bad-mouth or laugh at any idea, not even your own."

Write down every idea that is offered. Usually the group will identify one it likes best.

The creative ideas that come from brainstorming will amaze you. But what amazes even more is the way people feel about the idea they finally adopt. Somehow all tend to think of it as their own idea. This is true even though the original suggestion may have come from just one person.

Post-Meeting Communication

Communication after a meeting nurtures budding ownership. If the meeting itself did not begin the process, after-meeting work does not help. Devise sincere methods of reminding and thanking the members for their decision. Send notes thanking them for the time. In the note express excitement for the decision.

After the Meeting

At first this may seem hollow if you in fact would have preferred a different decision by the group. But remember what you really want: a group motivated to get something done, not just a good committee action lying dormant in some minutes somewhere. So thanking the members to reinforce their ownership is honest. Every time you talk to group members express thanks for their work and ideas.

Post-Meeting Duties

If the meeting has laid the ownership foundation, you can build on it when assigning the duties to carry out the decision. This is a critical step. The group can sense ownership, but this feeling can be destroyed by assigning duties improperly. There is a risk.

The board at Shulerville Church experienced this once. Pastor Jim was new and eager to make a good impression. The board had a great idea: "Let's have a church reunion banquet and ask all the past members and ministers to return as guests."

It *was* a good idea, and the board felt pride in it. They owned it. Pastor Jim dove into the project. For the next two months he contacted members and made all the arrangements. But the banquet flopped. Not even all the board members came. The board members had lost ownership, so they did not sell the idea to other church members. They thought the pastor would do so.

The lesson is, at the meeting or just afterward, assign duties to the members. This is not difficult if the members feel they own the idea. It is hard if they do not. Having people working on the project solidifies their ownership.

FOLLOW-UP WORK

An important part of managing a meeting is assigning follow-up work. The decision was to paint the church. Who lines up the workers? They decided to appoint a special youth task force.

Who decides who is on the committee and who calls the first meeting? The ideal is to have these decisions part of the committee action. The minutes report each action and report who is to carry out the decision. Remember that meetings *decide* things and people *do* things.

Sometimes it is not appropriate to name in a motion the person who is to do the work. Finding someone to oversee the church painting or to serve on a task force can take time. So a compromise is to assign decisions to board members. They do the follow-up work. In the matter of painting, the action might say, "Fifteen thousand dollars is for painting the church. Brother Don will find a project manager." This does not say Brother Don will manage the project; it says that he represents the board in the project. He is the contact point between the board and the project manager.

Functioning this way requires self-control. Most church leaders champion the motto, "If you want it done right, do it yourself." However, this demonstrates a lack of faith in the members and can cast a shadow over the church leadership's entire ministry.

There are several benefits to delegating the work. Delegation reinforces project ownership. It avoids overworking only a few people. It builds group commitment. Lastly, it builds church commitment.

When we assign work we must make sure that the tasks are expressed clearly. This is a weak board action: "The church board resolves to spruce up the church. Brother Brook is in charge." This directive is too general, and it is unfair to hook Brother Brook with such a poor job description. He is left with many unanswered questions: "How much can I spend? Do they mean the inside or the outside? Do they mean the building or the grounds?" Clear board actions ease the task of finding someone to do them.

Besides being stated clearly, good actions include sensible time frames. Many groups act as if a suitable goal is to get a certain job started before the next meeting. Recall the example of painting the church. The board assumed that Brother Don would find a project manager before its next meeting. That may be all right, but we must state time goals if the action requires a different time frame from the usual.

Suppose that in November the church votes to hire a college student for next summer's youth program. The action should make it clear that the interviews and hiring take place during March. This kind of a statement prevents misunderstandings.

SECRETARIES AND MINUTES

Often a committee's bylaws call for electing a secretary. Away with the idea that the secretary is a female! Elect anyone who has a laptop computer.

The secretary has two duties. First, he should be the committee's archivist. With research he should be able to answer questions such as "How did we handle this problem before?" or "When was the last time we painted the church?"

The second secretarial function is to keep the minutes. Often it is unwise for the secretary to do the actual writing of the minutes. If the secretary is to take part in the meeting along with the other members, it may be unfair to ask him to write the minutes. Perhaps there is someone else who can be brought in to take the minutes.

Minutes

Recording minutes is a real art. First the secretary must understand what the group expects. Does the committee want just a recording of the group's approved actions? Does it want the failed motions recorded? How about a paragraph summarizing the pros and cons offered for each action? Does the committee want a full account of the discussion?

The less that is required, the easier recording minutes becomes and the less trouble they can cause. However, the more you report, the more useful you are in carrying out the group's purpose. A full meeting account keeps absent members up to date. This reinforces action ownership. Also, with the full story one can easily discover the action's intent if there is a question later.

A good way to organize the minutes is this: Think about how problems and decisions flow through the committee. A problem comes to the chair's attention, and he or she places it on the agenda. This happens on a first-come-first-served basis or some other criterion. Then the group takes an action, and the secretary records it in the minutes. A good way to track this is for the chair to assign each problem a number as it enters the system. The chair includes items by number on the agenda, so that the secretary, in preparing the minutes, can identify by number the actions pertinent to each problem. This allows an easy cross-referencing to specific agenda items.

Consider an example. Deacon Don reports, "The roof is leaking, and I have obtained bids for a new one." The chair puts it on the agenda as item 96-6—that is, the sixth concern for 1996. The board thinks the bids are too high and votes to seek more. The minutes show this action under heading 96-6. At the next meeting the board accepts a bid. This action, too, is recorded under 96-6:

ITEM	DATE	ACTION
96-6	1-8-96	To ask Deacon Donnie to get more bids on replacing the roof.
96-6	2-10-96	To hire Ace Roofers for $18,000 to replace the roof. Deacon Donnie oversees this project.

This procedure is a departure from the standard practice of recording things in chronological order. It has the advantage of keeping together all the actions relating to a particular problem, and it also enables the group to keep track of unresolved problems.

EVALUATION

After the meeting, evaluate how well you did. An evaluation survey for meetings follows this chapter. It provides for evaluating both the chair and the group. It is to be used this way: Each member of the committee, including the chair, fills out the survey. Then the chair compiles and averages the members' responses, omitting his or her response out of the averages. The chair compares the group's averages with his or her own evaluation. This discloses how well others see the chair's effectiveness compared with his or her own perception, that is, how well the chair's actions match the group's expectations.

Other evaluation questions reveal what the members of the group think about themselves. Share the averages for these questions with the group.

Decision Evaluation

The committee should devise a system to evaluate their decision-making skills. One way is to set aside time for this, perhaps in June if the committee's function and schedule are related to the school year. (Many churches emphasize certain programs and ministries from September through May and suspend these activities during the summer months.) During this designated time the group surveys the decisions made in the previous calendar year. The secretary reads the major actions that have been decided by the group. The members discuss them and rate the decision quality on a scale from one to ten. Now they can see whether what they thought would happen with the actions actually happened. This is not Monday morning quarterbacking; it is more like a football team's watching tapes of their most recent game. They are looking for ways to play better.

MEETING SELF-EVALUATION

Instructions: Read each question and circle the score that you feel is appropriate. Then mark with a star the score that you think we should be shooting for.

1. *Were agendas and advance materials sent out on time and in an acceptable form?*

1	2	3	4	5	6	7	8	9	10
No									Yes

2. *Were goals well defined?*

1	2	3	4	5	6	7	8	9	10
No									Yes

3. *How successful was the meeting in reaching the goals?*

1	2	3	4	5	6	7	8	9	10
Poor									Good

4. *How well did the chair keep the group goal directed?*

1	2	3	4	5	6	7	8	9	10
Poor									Good

5. *How well did the group stay goal directed?*

1	2	3	4	5	6	7	8	9	10
Poor									Good

6. *How well did the chair manage time?*

1	2	3	4	5	6	7	8	9	10
Poor									Good

7. *How well did the group manage time?*

1	2	3	4	5	6	7	8	9	10
Poor									Good

8. *Was the chair fair in governing the process (e.g., calling on people, following Robert's Rules of Order)?*

1	2	3	4	5	6	7	8	9	10
No									Yes

9. *Did members talk openly, and were views stated clearly?*

1	2	3	4	5	6	7	8	9	10
No									Yes

10. *Did the group put the finishing touches on the decisions (e.g., work was assigned, motions were stated clearly)?*

1	2	3	4	5	6	7	8	9	10
No									Yes

11. *Are the members committed to the committee?*

1	2	3	4	5	6	7	8	9	10
No									Yes

12. *Did anyone dominate the committee?*

1	2	3	4	5	6	7	8	9	10
No									Yes

13. *Was the meeting room satisfactory?*

1	2	3	4	5	6	7	8	9	10
No									Yes

14. *How do your rate the meeting overall?*

1	2	3	4	5	6	7	8	9	10
Bad									Good

Chapter 8

Games Committees Play

Pastor Jim is awake and angry. It is 2:00 A.M., but he does not care. Usually, when he is angry and wakeful, he becomes more upset because of his sleeplessness. Not tonight. Tonight he ignores the time. Brother Ebenezer really got to him tonight. This is what happened.

The board meeting started innocently enough. It was expected that one major item would fill the entire meeting. The church was deciding what size the new church building should be. The problem: The church is growing rapidly, so the congregation needs to account for future needs. It can realistically afford only so much debt. Now, if the church keeps growing at its current pace, building a much larger facility is a wise course. It will serve the new members well, and they will help to pay off the debt. However, a slower rate of growth would burden the present membership with an oversized building and too large a debt.

Pastor Jim was prepared. He had met with architects, builders, and bankers to weigh all the factors. He made charts showing several scenarios regarding growth, space, and debt. He sent each member an agenda and an explanation of the problem. He felt quite satisfied about all the work and time he had put into the matter.

As chair of the meeting, Pastor Jim called for the reading of the minutes of the previous meeting. At that meeting the board asked him to conduct the annual evaluation of the church secretary. But Jim forgot about it. After the minutes were read, someone asked Jim about the evaluation.

Pastor Jim responded, "I haven't had time. I am really busy with the building plans."

Brother John said, "I know that the building is hard work, but we really need this evaluation. We want to know how she is doing."

"I will try to do it by next month's meeting."

Brother Ebenezer asked, "What do you mean, you 'will try'?"

"I meant that if I can find the time, I'll do it," Jim said.

"Doesn't this board mean anything to you?"

"Yes, I want you to be—"

"Didn't we hire you? If you feel that we are putting too many demands on your time—if you can't handle the work we want done—maybe we should get someone else."

The other board members were silent.

Brother Ebenezer tended to view himself as a down-to-business, hard-driving, no-ifs-and-or-buts kind of person. He took pride in his holding-the-line view of life.

Pastor Jim felt bad—a weird sort of bad, not a "wise" bad that comes from having hard work dismissed or plans messed up. He felt a "foolish" bad, such as one feels when getting a traffic ticket or when edged out in checkout lane at the supermarket. Before he could stop himself, he blurted out a response to Brother Ebenezer.

"You slimy old goat! You have caused me nothing but trouble since I met you. You are the stupidest . . ."

Initially there was a sense of elation at Pastor Jim's standing up for himself. But he was wrong.

Brother Ebenezer nearly burst a blood vessel. Just two seconds earlier he had been feeling proud. Now the pastor was calling him "slimy," a "goat," and "stupid." Raging, Ebenezer stormed from the room.

Should we feel sorry for Brother Ebenezer? At the risk of sounding too psychoanalytical, I suggest that people like Brother Ebenezer welcome rage. There may be a kind of pleasure that comes from raging. For the next few weeks Ebenezer's rage will fill an otherwise shallow life. And Sister Ebenezer will sense relief at having his rage directed toward someone else.

Pastor Jim is the person we should worry about. What caused such an outburst? Jim is a good guy. His rage is neither logical nor spiritually reasonable. Brother Ebenezer did not deserve that outburst. So what went wrong?

It is three o'clock, and Jim is settling down. He had been pacing, but now is sitting in his dark study looking at the numbers on the VCR clock.

Jim's anger toward Brother Ebenezer has evaporated. Now he is angry with himself. It is not a harmful self-anger, but a beneficial type. It entails the self-reflection that leads to improvement. Then it hits Jim: He is not angry because Ebenezer is a complaining, unhappy, obstructionist crab. Jim is angry because the little boy in him got him into trouble. The little-boy trait had lashed out in a childish way at Brother Ebenezer, who was acting in a parental way.

The recognition that this is what happened makes Jim feel better. His behavior was not caused by an uncontrolled, wicked heart; it resulted from a character trait that has to be healed by some hard work.

Jim prays for freedom from falling back into parent-child roles with people. He frames an apology for Brother Ebenezer. He will deliver it tomorrow and at the next board meeting.

He lies down on the couch in his study and sleeps until late the next morning.

TRANSACTIONAL ANALYSIS

The phenomenon that is besetting Jim is nothing new. It has been defined since the mid-1960s in an approach to interpersonal relationships called "transactional analysis," or "T.A." Two best-selling books in particular brought T.A. to public awareness: *Games People Play* and *I'm OK You're OK*.[1]

The books explain relationships in terms of people's speaking from the Child, the Parent, or the Adult ego—states that exist simultaneously within each person. The Child is the person's rebellious, I-want-my-own-way part. The Parent is the person's legalistic, condemnatory part. The Adult is the rational, let's-solve-the-problem part. In the Christian sense the Adult is the person's mature, Spirit-led part.

Suppose I drop a water glass and it breaks. Laughing about what a fool I am or worrying about my wife's anger over the incident is the Child in me. Becoming angry is my Parent. Saying "I need a mop" is my Adult.

The goal of transactional analysis is to help people have an Adult-controlled psyche. When a person's relationships and psyche are functioning the way psychologists believe they should be, it means "you're okay and I'm okay."

Why should a book on committee meetings resurrect pop psychology that is two decades old? The reason is that transactional analysis gives insight into committee behavior.

A committee has a subconsciousness—the veiled mental process that operates behind the group's activities. It is its own mind, distinct from the group members' minds. Committee members play games in this subconscious arena, and the players do not know they are playing them.

The story at the beginning of this chapter gives evidence

---

[1]Eric Berne, *Games People Play* (New York: Grove Press, 1964), and Thomas Harris, *I'm OK You're OK* (New York: Harper & Row, 1967).

of game-playing. During the meeting both Brother Ebenezer and Pastor Jim felt that they were dealing on an Adult (rational) level. But Brother Ebenezer was acting in the Parent mode, and this pulled Pastor Jim into a Child response. A subconscious desire to avoid making hard decisions about the size of the building fueled this process.

Management people[2] took the concepts of the transactional analysis model and applied them to committee dynamics. People play committee games from an "I'm not okay but you are" position. This is the typical self-image people acquire from their upbringing. This feeling leads to many different games that fit into several categories.

WHAT A GOOD BOY AM I

In the first set of games, players overcome their "I am not okay" feelings by advancing themselves. The first What-a-Good-Boy game is Today's Miracles.

Today's Miracles Game

We often see this game being played during report time on the agenda. Suppose the Sunday school director gives a glowing presentation. There are no problems to report—just peace, love, and hard work. She only mentions problems that show the great way she handled them.

This game can be seen in other ways in churches. There is a contrast between a proper positive Christianity and only giving a department's good side by hiding weaknesses and failures.

The How-Hard-We-Have-It Game

Members play this game along with the Today's Miracles game. The players enhance their images by showing the

---

[2]See Richard Dunsing, *You and I Have Simply Got to Stop Meeting This Way* (New York: American Management Assn., 1976), pp. 33–39, and Dorothy Jongeward, *Everybody Wins: Transactional Analysis Applied to Organizations* (Reading, Mass.: Addison Wesley, 1976).

struggles they overcame in giving such good leadership. "We really had a hard time getting enough Sunday school teachers. It just seems people are not willing to teach anymore. But I finally got enough, and everything is working great."

The How-Hard-We-Work Game

This game is similar to How Hard We Have It, but it focuses on the difficulty of the work, not the responsibility. It spins off on the Protestant work ethic that says the harder we work the more righteous ("okay") we are. So if I have spent hours on some project for the church, I am okay. Even if the work is not needed, I am okay for working long and hard.

The Sunday school director who plays this game says, "This job is killing me. I spent two days this week down here getting the materials straight."

The Under-the-Rug Game

Hiding problems and mistakes is the purpose of this game. The more we hide, the higher our score. Players may refer coyly to the things hidden under someone else's rug. However, yanking away someone else's rug to expose the problems is against the rules.

This game is difficult for newcomers in a group to play. They lack insight into the situation. They easily blunder under someone else's rug. Also, since they do not know what is under others' rugs, they are anxious about whether they can hide things under their own rugs. Often a mature player lets a newcomer know "what is really going on."

BLAME-AND-BASH GAMES

Games in the second category are more brutal. Those who play them feel frantic in their "I am not okay but you are" feelings. They feel that to counter these feelings by building themselves up is useless, so they work to put others down.

The If-It-Were-Not-for-Them Game

The people who play this game say, "If it were not for so and so, we would have done so and so." They shift the blame for failure away from themselves. The player blames someone inside or outside the group for the group's failures. He or she does this, not so much to keep from being blamed as to build up his or her own self-esteem.

This tactic dampens the mood of the entire group. It prevents the group from moving ahead and making decisions. Everyone loses in this game.

The Blemish Game

This game is very subtle and can only be played by true masters. The point is to blemish the report or the committee's actions. These players avoid causing any real, long-term damage; they simply knock the shine off the committee's work.

Suppose the Sunday school director is reporting on the success of the retarded children's program. The director says, "We're having a good time with our 'Special Children' Sunday school class. We have a good group, and we are very blessed that Joyce is leading them. She is a real professional with retarded children and is doing a great job."

Blemish responds, "Didn't I hear that little Freddy blackened Sue's eye last Sunday?"

Notice that Blemish's attack is not direct. The question simply rubs the shine off the report. Somehow this helps Blemish deal with the "not okay" feelings. Blemish pros often play this game in newly formed groups or groups brought together briefly to receive a report.

The Shoot-Out Game

"Shoot-outs" occur when one player attacks a player's weak spot, and that player retorts with a countershot. This tactic enables the combatants to avoid dealing with the committee's real problems. Groups that work together frequently are likely to play this game best, because the players learn one other's weaknesses and "hot buttons."

Stopping the game is hard, because the players will resist the efforts. The incident with Pastor Jim and Brother Ebenezer illustrates this.

Often the exchange of gunfire leaves both players wounded. However, this is not a big concern, especially if it happens often. Some people find the anger aroused in the confrontation to be a stimulant—something like sanctified drug abuse. Many conservative Christians frown on watching violent movies, boxing, or taking stimulating drugs, but they enjoy arguing and becoming angry at meetings. They ignore the inconsistency. Not dealing with their anger or resentment about such things as family life, they vent their feelings in a committee meeting.

The "Gotcha" Game

The Gotchas lack the poise of the Blemishes. The game is simply this: You goof up, and we jump up and down on you. "Gotcha" is especially effective when played against ministers. If the minister has faults, then we cannot be quite so bad as we thought.

Not surprisingly, "Gotcha" undoes many called to the ministry. Every pastor can tell horror stories about how he or she fell victim to this game. It is little comfort to know that players play from their insecurities and not because of real pastoral weakness.

The Zip-Zap Game

Zip-Zap is a milder version of Shoot-Out. Taking turns, everyone shoots at almost everyone else. It is not as deadly as Shoot-Out, since each player knows that his or her shot will come. So there are not as many hard feelings. Group members play this game on the cliff near the Chaos game.

The Chaos Game

This book does not seek to explain the Chaos Game's rules, because there are no rules and anything can and does happen.

PITY GAMES

Games in the third category work among those who neither build themselves up nor tear others down. These players deal with their "I'm not okay but you are" feelings by saying, "If I am not okay and you are, you owe me. I might as well get the most out of this bad situation."

The Kick-Me Game

In this game, players set themselves up for a kicking, then some obliging person gives a boot. That boot reinforces the first player's insecurities and allows him or her to withdraw from the group work. Though the first player may physically be present in the committee, he or she feels no responsibility or need to contribute. The kicked players lose because they wither as leaders. The rest of the group lose because they don't have the benefit of the kicked players' wisdom and help. The members also feel guilty for being party to the bullying.

The Breathless-Boss Game

This is a solitary game sometimes played by ministers or other church leaders. These players portray themselves as harried but in control. They use their tight schedules as an excuse to neglect people's needs. We can spot the game in the account that follows.

The minister rushes into the meeting room a few minutes late. He looks at his watch and mumbles something about such-and-such a problem tying him up. There is prayer and the reading of the minutes. Then the minister says, "I want to skip the financial report for this meeting and discuss the new church building."

The treasurer who stayed up last night preparing the

report mildly protests. The minister says, "I am sorry, Mary. I meant to call you, but I am just so busy." Here the minister is using his breathless pace as an excuse for his insensitivity to the group members for being late and to Mary for not calling and preempting her responsibility.

OPTIMIZER GAMES

The fourth category has subtle "I am not okay" games in which the players say, "If you are so great, you should act like it." These players force the group toward a standard of perfection that no one can achieve.

The We-Need-So-and-So Game

The people who play this game obstruct the committee's progress by claiming, for example, that certain information is missing, an expert opinion is lacking, or the topic is outside the committee's frame of reference. Suppose a parent committee is responsible for setting up a church school. The discussion turns to curriculum. Brother Otis, the optimizer, says, "This group should not discuss curriculum. This group needs some teachers."

That is perhaps a true statement, but it can be a game tactic that taints or sabotages all future talk of curriculum. It excuses Brother Otis if the group makes a curriculum error: "Didn't I say we needed some teachers working on this?"

Some optimizing suggestions may be correct, and this makes counteracting the game difficult. All that members can do is review the situation to see if the claim—the suggested approval or information—is truly needed. Sometimes the committee can proceed even if the claims have some validity. They could continue to work in the understanding that an expert will review their actions. Or perhaps the committee can make a responsible decision based on the best information at hand. Or maybe they can make tentative and alternative decisions based on the possible scenarios that new information would suggest.

The Control Game

Some people deal with the "I am not okay but you are" feelings by controlling situations. This control may be blatant, as when a member jockeys to become chair of the committee. Or the control may be more more subtle: simply talk a lot.

The controlling optimizer exerts the slyest form of control. No matter what the suggestion, the controlling optimizer adds the finishing touches. This seems harmless, but it does entail hazards.

Twenty-year-old Eric attended a church meeting on how to evangelize Shulerville. A novice when it comes to church committees, he said, "I used to work at the Medical Center Hospital. I am sure they will let me put tracts in the waiting rooms. I know where they are like the back of my hand. I could cover every waiting room in twenty minutes. I'll do it every Saturday afternoon."

The controlling optimizer spoke up, "You need to take someone with you so they can learn how to do it." This sounds harmless enough, but Eric ultimately never took the first tract to the hospital. His interest died, because what was a simple project suddenly became complicated. Now in order to do it right he had to find a partner, arrange a time to meet, and who knows what else. Eric had wanted to make a quick stop at the hospital. The optimizer's comment took the project's ownership away from Eric. And since he would not do it "right," Eric did not do it at all.

Little comments can be more hurtful than they at first appear.

MISCELLANEOUS GAMES

There are several games that do not fall into any of the foregoing categories.

Games Committees Play

The Better-Safe-Than-Sorry Game

This strategy may not truly be a game in the sense that it is played in silence. Management research[3] suggests that with this phenomenon group members hesitate to speak up for fear of reprisals. For example, the youth minister may not express an opinion contrary to the pastor's lest the pastor retaliate in some way later on. This hesitancy may linger even when there are no supporting facts. The pastor may be a very gentle, open-minded person who sincerely seeks guidance. Nevertheless, the fear of reprisal persists.

This kind of apprehension can be strong when a committee member happens to be an employee of another member. It makes no difference whether or not there has ever been any experience of punishment for not supporting the boss. But the fantasy gives the player an excuse for not contributing.

The Meeting-Addict Game

We all know people who are meeting addicts. They address their "I m not okay but you are" feelings by attending an inordinate number of meetings. The need to bustle from one meeting to another may arise from an effort to bolster the self-image by "doing something." Sadly, meetings do not accomplish real work. Meetings accomplish many things, but the follow up to the decisions is where the real work gets done. The meeting addicts are just fooling themselves.

STIR-FRIED GAMES

Identifying games is hard. Only when players play them in their most exaggerated forms do the games become visible. The reason is that several members may be playing different games at the same time. The bullies are playing the Gotcha Game while Pity Patty is playing Kick Me. Almost everyone is playing Zip Zap, and the chair is playing Breathless Boss.

---

[3]"The Abilene Paradox: The Management of Agreement," *Organizational Dynamics* (Summer 1974).

Knowing about these games can help cure a committee's game playing. One person's games brings out another's. When others do something to increase their stature, it brings out our "I am not okay but you are" feelings. So my games bring out yours, which in turn intensify mine. And so on. If we are playing the How-Hard-We-Have-It Game, someone may join the game by agreeing with us and saying how hard they have it. Or a less kind person may thwart us by playing Blemish.

GAME CURES

Several factors keep the games in their boxes on the game shelf. We don't need to know which game is being played in order to cure it. Pointing out games as games only worsens the problem—and is itself a game. This gives the message that we are better because we have such great insight, while the players are worse because they are playing the games.

The first step toward a cure is to know what causes games in us: "I'm not okay but you are" feelings. We must stop playing games ourselves. When only one person refuses to play games, it greatly reduces game playing overall. One person's confidence and security provide a safe haven in which others can find shelter.

The secular world has invented several devices to bring out the desired "I'm okay you're okay" feelings. These include direct talk about the feelings and ignoring the game playing. If someone does not enter into the game, the players quickly stop.

Christian groups should give people the chance to fail and be supported. Church business meetings should be an emotional haven. Helping others overcome their "not okay" feelings is the quickest way to overcome our own. The gospel is the gospel because it provides the solution to "I'm not okay" feelings. Feeling "okay" is easy when we know that God sees us as important.

Chapter 9

Groupthink

It is Shulerville's major landmark. If you are telling someone the way to the mall you say, "Go two blocks down Main Street and turn at the ugly church on the left." It is indeed the city's ugliest building. What a shame! Not that it was cheap to build: The church spent a fortune constructing it. Not that it was built poorly: The builder followed the plans exactly. Not that it was hastily designed: The building committee spent hours working on each detail.

The church's pastor, Bill, nearly quit the Shulerville Ministerial Association over it. At every meeting he was teased about it. Finally the association president told members, "Use your Christian graces and leave him alone."

When Pastor Jim's congregation started their building program, he invited Pastor Bill to lunch and tactfully asked, "I really don't know about bringing this up. It is sort of embarrassing, and I don't want to hurt your feelings. But would you mind—well, would you mind talking about—you know, um—your church building. I don't think it's all that bad, but I want to learn from your—um, you know—your mistake—not really your mistake, but if there are any pointers you can give me from your church building ordeal. Not that it was an ordeal. I mean your incident—no, not incident—I mean your experience. What can you tell me?"

Pastor Jim had not groped for words so badly since the time Brother Ebenezer's granddaughter asked if he was the ass during the children's story one Palm Sunday.

Pastor Bill took a deep sigh. He had a fairly good outlook about the whole matter. It seems that about once a month some young pastor would buy him lunch and ask the same question. He made a mental note: Make a handout sheet about what went wrong; maybe I can get it published.

Pastor Bill explained, "The building committee made all the decisions. They are the church's brightest and most talented people. We prayed before every meeting to seek God's guidance. There was no powerful member who forced his will on us. We worked on each decision until we all agreed. The spirit among us was great. There was no bickering. We worked as a great team. Everyone cooperated. In fact, we were sorry when we had finished the job because we had grown so close to each other. The problem was this: We simply made bad decisions."

How could twelve very talented and bright people make such dumb decisions about that church building? The question has been asked before and will be asked again. The answer may be "groupthink."

THE BAY OF PIGS

On a warm spring day in 1961, fourteen hundred brave Cuban exiles invaded Cuba at an inlet called the Bay of Pigs. The United States Navy, Air Force, and Central Intelligence Agency were to support the invasion. But every carefully laid plan failed, and within three days about two hundred invaders were dead and the rest were sent into Premier Fidel

Castro's prison camps. The United States came under criticism from major allies. Worldwide, protest rallies condemned the Goliath United States for beating up on a tiny neighbor.[1]

A committee had decided on and laid the plans for the Cuban invasion. This was no committee of lightweights. These are the committee members and the positions they held before joining the Kennedy administration:

Dean Rusk	Head, Rockefeller Foundation
Robert McNamara	President, Ford Motor Co.
Douglas Dillon	Secretary of the Treasury
McGeorge Bundy	Dean of Arts and Sciences, Harvard University
Arthur Schlesinger	Historian, Harvard University

Joining this core group were the Joint Chiefs of Staff and the top State Department experts on the Caribbean.

The group decided on the invasion of Cuba by fourteen hundred men secretly supported by American firepower. This was designed to look like an internal revolution. Castro brought twenty thousand soldiers against the invaders in one day. Everyone who studied the decision afterward has called it foolish. Even the committee members now say it was a big mistake. How could such a smart group make such a dumb decision?

GROUPTHINK

Political scientists looked at the Bay of Pigs and other fiascoes and came up with the concept of groupthink. Groupthink means that decision-making groups will work at keeping harmony among the members even at the cost of impaired judgment. Groupthink leads the members unconsciously to share many illusions and norms collectively. These illusions hinder clear thinking and reality testing. For example, the Bay of Pigs committee believed that the

---

[1]The concept of groupthink and the Bay of Pigs example are from the book *Victims of Groupthink* by Irving Janis (Boston: Houghton Mifflin, 1972). I recommend this book for interesting reading on your next vacation.

fourteen hundred invaders could take on Castro's two hundred thousand soldiers successfully. The committee knew the size of Castro's army before the invasion began, but it operated under the illusion that the army would be weak, confused, and disloyal. Groupthink caused a group fantasy that ignored reality. There are several other groupthink fantasies of which to be aware.

Group Subconsciousness

The fantasies and other groupthink features do not operate on a conscious level. Without getting too mystical, we can say that a committee has a mind of its own. This mind works apart from the minds of the individual committee members. This mind works in the background without any member's being aware of its methods. In this mind groupthink operates.

An example will make this clear. One groupthink facet to be discussed later is that members silence other members who do not agree with the group. Done in an openly hostile way, this is not groupthink. Suppose one member screams at another, "You always complain about what we are doing. Would you please shut up!" This is not groupthink. Nor is it as harmful as groupthink.

Groupthink is more subtle. It is not a case of greedy, power-hungry members' getting their own way. It operates below the surface without anyone's conscious aid. It is a natural, almost gentle, process emerging from the way we relate to others. This natural process is very strong among Christians who want harmony with each other.

GROUPTHINK FANTASIES

There are three groupthink fantasies. Analysts say that identifying groupthink fantasies when they are happening is difficult. Like all good fantasies, they seem real until they end. We see them as fantasies only after they have inflicted their damage by causing a bad decision. We see them only after the invasion fails, the church building turns out ugly, or the main committee laughs at the subcommittee's report.

Reflect on your committee work. Try to spot occasions when these fantasies have hurt your group's decisions.

The We-Are-Good Fantasy

The first groupthink fantasy focuses on the committee's self-esteem. The Bay of Pigs committee members admit that they viewed themselves as almost invincible. They felt this way solely because of the virtue in what they were doing. They felt so invincible that they sent fourteen hundred exiles against two hundred thousand soldiers. This high group self-esteem comes from the "we" feeling and the security nurtured in membership in a powerful committee. The fantasy says that nothing can stop this bright, wise, moral group. Members see themselves as fallible individually, but infallible as a group. Combat units and athletic teams use this natural group dynamic to great advantage. It is deadly, however, for committees that have to make crucial decisions.

This "supergroup," as Irving Janis calls it, views itself, like Superman, as able to "leap tall buildings in a single bound." The supergroup thinks it can handle any trial. It ignores its weaknesses and so does not explore options in case it has made a poor decision. It anticipates that it will handle the problems as they arise.

We have all seen this phenomenon in committees, no matter how important or unimportant the group is. Consider the church music committee. When they are together the members can easily get the idea that as a group they have the greatest wisdom for directing the church music program.

The We-Are-Good fantasy is strong in Christian committees. After all: "Didn't we pray before the meeting? Didn't we say 'God bless our decisions'? Aren't we all Christians? Didn't we feel the Spirit as we made our judgments?"

All these factors improve decision making. But the Devil easily counterfeits them all. The Spirit euphoria that we feel in a committee may be merely group dynamics. So, as we are commonly told in Christian teaching, feelings are no guide to what is best.

The They-Are-Bad Fantasy

The second groupthink fantasy can be called They Are
Bad. All the factors that make a group think they are good also
leds them to feel that all foes are very bad. The Bay of Pigs
committee honestly felt that Fidel Castro was a "weak,
hysteric leader whose army was ready to defect."[2]

The They-Are-Bad Fantasy can appear in strange ways.
This group dynamic can be so strong that the "They" in
"They are bad" is completely fictional. The committee debate
refers to the mysterious "They" like this: *"They* will never
buy this" or *"They* will be upset when they hear about this."

"They" can be almost any outsider. This fantasy often
emerges when one committee is accountable to another or
must have another's consent before its decisions can be
carried out. Vilifying the other committee's motives is easy.

Suppose that the youth committee must get approval
from the church board for its major projects. As the youth
committee is establishing its program the members may
begin viewing the church board as villains who don't care
about the church youth: "Those old fogies will never let us do
this." Also, the church board may view the youth committee
as "liberals lowering the church's standards." Yet each group
may actually view caring for the youth and upholding the
standards as top priorities.

This "We are good and they are bad" illusion is a group
dynamic that may arise quite naturally in any committee. Be
alert for it at anytime when one group is accountable to
another group. Left unattended, this fantasy can lead to
splinter groups and factions in a church.

The Consensus Fantasy

The next fantasy within groupthink is the Consensus
Fantasy. This fantasy assumes two things. First, if the
committee members reach a unanimous decision, it must be
the best. This alone is not hazardous; but group members

---

[2]Janis, *Victims of Groupthink,* 38.

begin to trust the consensus instead of doing their own critical thinking and reality testing. "Everyone agrees on this, so it must be all right."

Arthur Schlesinger, one of planners of the Bay of Pigs invasion, said, "Had one senior adviser opposed the adventure, I believe that Kennedy would have canceled it." There is irony in this, because each member has since reported having had serious doubts about going ahead with the mission.[3]

Churches experience this phenomenon. At a board meeting everyone seems behind you on an issue and later it seems that no one is supporting you. The week after a unanimous vote, people are privately expressing their concerns about the action. Or after a decision backfires, the best defense that can be made was that "everyone agreed."

ISOLATIONISM

All these fantasies result in one major feature that characterizes groupthink. As a committee's groupthink grows, its isolation grows. If "we" are good and "they" are bad, we should keep our debate secret. Committees bound by groupthink cherish their decisions as a mother cherishes her baby. These groups prefer to keep their ideas inside the group. The group gets elitist feelings that communicate that they are a special group, their decisions are special, and no common folks should see them.

Granted, certain matters are so sensitive that they must be handled discreetly. This is the familiar "national security" line that the federal government often uses. But within churches this excuse for keeping a group's activities secret is often just a result of groupthink. "If this ever gets out, *they* will shred it." Perhaps making the activities public will disarm those very fears.

---

[3]Janis, *Victims of Groupthink*, 39.

MAVERICKS

Another striking feature of groupthink relates to mavericks. Studies suggest that dissenting members feel group pressure to conform and preserve harmony. Groups prod members to silence if their views conflict with the consensus. This pressure is very subtle. It is not a case of one member telling another, "Be quiet." The group does the prodding with only a little hostility and in such a positive way that the now-silent dissident feels good about the love and belongingness. This pressure grows stronger as the final decision comes closer.

Strangely enough, groups often do this prodding with humor. Committee members unwittingly use lighthearted bantering and joking to goad a questioning member into the fold. A serious question that draws a humorous retort clearly shows that this is happening.

Christianity focuses on harmony. First Peter 3:8 says, "Finally, all of you, live in harmony with one another." But we must remember that true harmony comes from God's indwelling, not from squeezing everyone into the same mold. Conformity is not synonymous with harmony.

MIND GUARDS

Sometimes someone appoints himself or herself as the group's mind guard. This person seeks out committee members at breaks or after meetings and works toward preserving group harmony or protecting the group leader. Mind guards also protect the group from information that does not support the emerging decision or information that counters the group's "we versus them" mindset. Take note of members who appear to be controlling the group's information flow.

Committees of Christians are often beset with mind guards. Matthew 5:9 says, "Blessed are the peacemakers, for they will be called sons of God." James 3:18 says, "Peacemakers who sow in peace raise a harvest of righteousness." This biblical counsel mandates efforts to develop harmony in a group, and members working privately can assist the group toward this end and toward a good decision. But the process can be unwittingly corrupted. Often truth is better than harmony.

Do not look upon mind guards and advocates of conformity as malicious evildoers. These strategies arise from natural group processes rooted in the group subconscious. They are subtle, and people who honestly want the best decision fall victim to them.

TOKEN DISSIDENTS

A curious figure in groupthink is the token dissident. A committee may be operating in perfect harmony—victim of the fantasies already discussed. All the members may be perfectly in the fold so that there is no dissent. But this little nirvana makes members uncomfortable. Everything is too good. Now there emerges the token dissident.

The token dissident raises mild objections, and the other members shoot the objections down. This causes warm feelings about the thorough job the members are doing. Since everyone knows that the token dissident is really in the group fold, no one presses for conformity. We can observe token dissidents whenever someone raises opposition in a discussion. Someone will address the opposition mildly, and then a vote is taken and it is unanimous. The token dissident has voted contrary to his verbal position. If this happens very often in your committee, then groupthink is working, and there is a token dissident.

PERSONAL DOUBTS

The capacity for groupthink to handle personal doubts is interesting. As we noted earlier, after the Bay of Pigs fiasco, every committee member reported having had personal doubts about the plan's wisdom. Most said that they figured that if so many other bright people thought it was such a good idea, then their own doubts were misplaced.

In committee meetings, many honest, usually outspoken people will hold their tongues to avoid creating disharmony.

They fear rejection at appearing foolish. The Bay of Pigs committee members feared looking too liberal or gutless.

In the church this capacity for stifling personal doubts can be harmful. Humility is a Christian virtue, but some people confuse humility with inferiority. Putting ourselves down so that we fear to express an opinion is not humility. We may be hindering God's work by not speaking up in the group.

CURES FOR GROUPTHINK

Solving the problems of groupthink is difficult, because groupthink arises from a natural desire for group cooperation. Just as when cancer infiltrates a vital organ, the cure may be more dangerous than the disease. The suggested remedies should be applied skillfully. Too much medicine may kill the patient.

Remedy 1

The group should select several members as official "devil's advocates." These members seek to challenge consensus and identify weaknesses in proposed actions. This is not to be done in a contentious way, of course; the purpose is to make sure that every aspect of a proposal has been explored so as to reduce the potential for unwelcome consequences of an action.

Remedy 2

At least one meeting should allow time for identifying all the drawbacks to a decision. Before this meeting assign half the group to argue against the decision. This subgroup should include people who were early advocates of it. During this reality testing, every member should express at least one doubt or criticism of the proposed action.

Remedy 3

Invite outside experts or capable co-workers who are not part of the core group to attend every meeting. Have them attend in rotation to avoid pulling them into the group dynamics. They should challenge the core group's thinking. There is a drawback in this procedure: Some time will be spent reviewing the history of the decision making.

Remedy 4

In the group's early stages, divide it into two subgroups with a mandate for each group to come up with a recommendation. Then reunite the subgroups, look at their solutions, and work out any conflicts or neglected issues.

Remedy 5

Assign each member to talk with trusted colleagues about the discussions and report their results to the group.

Remedy 6

On major issues, the committee should set up two separate groups that will deal with the same problem. Then a third group (without members from the other groups) should resolve conflicts and choose the better option. This strategy is becoming very popular in the business world.

Remedy 7

Organizational leaders not sitting on the committee should be impartial about its final decisions. Respected leaders expressing a desired outcome can inhibit free and open discussion and reduce the likelihood of achieving a successful action.

Remedy 8

Committee leaders should prompt—even force—members to express their doubts. Compel members to debate. Sometimes, when one person has been arguing steadfastly for one action and another is arguing steadfastly against it, the chair should force a fifteen-minute role switch. Each advocate would argue the other's position. Suppose someone suggests an idea and no one is arguing against it. The chair can divide the committee into a pro group and a con group and thereby ensure that negative aspects of a decision will be aired. A

A GROUPTHINK QUESTIONNAIRE

Groupthink can appear in virtually every committee. This questionnaire will help you detect how it is manifest in your group.

1. Does the committee consider several plausible solutions before selecting one, or does the first proposal get readily adopted?

2. Does the committee list carefully all the drawbacks for the emerging solution?

3. When a drawback is identified, does the committee discuss a strategy for dealing with the drawback?

4. Is there any opposition in the group?

5. Is the opposition viewed in a bad light?

6. Do committee members refer to an unidentified "they"?

7. How do members treat maverick opinions?

8. Do maverick opinions ever change the group's thinking?

9. Does the group have a mind guard?

10. Does the group have a token dissenter?

11. Does the group joke a lot, especially with serious suggestions?

12. Are the group's decisions always unanimous?

13. Is the group afraid to let its decisions be made public?

14. Does group membership manifest shades of elitism?

15. Are outsiders welcome or invited to discuss the group's decisions?

---

creative chair can improve the group's decisions by insisting on debate.

These remedies fight the natural forces working toward harmony within the group. The committee members and especially the chair must stir up some discord to combat groupthink's harmful effects. This requires skillful balancing. A group with too much harmony or with too much discord will make bad decisions. The wise chair manages these qualities carefully.

Chapter 10

Baptized Rules of Order

Brother Ebenezer is in his glory. The meeting is in chaos. It all started so innocently.

There was a long agenda. The meeting began with prayer. The finance report was positive. The youth minister gave a good report about the recent youth retreat. Then Pastor Jim said, "We really need to get the kids a VCR and TV so we can show movies. Right now we borrow someone's every time we show a movie."

"No!" Brother Ebenezer disputed. "Those VCRs are the Devil's. Sure you will say we will get only wholesome movies. But compromise will begin. First you will get PG movies, then PG-13 movies; then NR-17. Who knows where it ends? I don't think we should get one."

Sister Sarah chimed in, "My children have a VCR, and I don't see anything wrong with it as long as you control it."

Brother John said, "I got one, and my children are always slipping something by me on it."

Sister Susie interjected, "I don't think they are as bad as those TV video games!"

"What's wrong with TV video games?"

"Nothing is wrong. They just waste a lot of time when the kids could be doing something better—like working on their Boy Scout badges."

"If they are boys. Remember, we don't let the girls into Boy Scouts."

"Well, I think we should. It is unfair making the girls feel as if they are excluded from anything."

Before long the entire board crumbled into little groups, each arguing about letting the girls into the Boy Scouts. Some wanted to let them in. Others favored letting them in, but giving the organization a new name such as "The Pathfinders." Others were angry about ruining "an American institution." Still others said that their colleagues have to "wake up and smell the coffee. This is nearly the twenty-first century!" (No one was exactly sure what that meant.)

Finally Pastor Jim started shouting to stop people from arguing. By that time, people were thinking that talking about such routine things as VCRs when the girls' welfare is at stake was silly. Those in favor of keeping the girls out of the Boy Scouts thought the meeting needed to stick to the agenda. But those wanting the girls in the Boy Scouts thought Pastor Jim was fighting against them by cutting off debate. So the board voted against getting the VCR.

RULES OF ORDER

The Shulerville Church board needed some rules of order. These are the guidelines and procedures used to run a meeting. We will call them simply "rules." Rules have several benefits. They—

—Improve a meeting's fruitfulness. They move the group through the decision-making process. They encourage the members to stay on the current topic. Rules of order gave

Pastor Jim a way to handle members who were wandering from the topic.

—Ensure that the group practices democracy. They prevent any faction from controlling the decision-making process. They keep a minority group from overpowering the majority.

—Ensure that the minority group can speak to an issue.

—Reduce the potential for unfair actions by the chair.

—Give all members equal opportunity to bring relevant items before the group.

History

The history of the rules of order makes good reading. The parliamentary rules began with the British Parliament and had developed over centuries of legislative give and take. Thomas Jefferson used Parliament's rules as a springboard when he drafted the rules of procedure for the U.S. Congress. However, these rules—also called "parliamentary procedure"—do not serve smaller decision-making groups as well as they serve legislative bodies.

In 1876, Major Henry Robert modified Congress's rules and developed Robert's Rules of Order. He said he wanted a set of rules that make church meetings fruitful and fair.[1] (One wonders whether somewhere there is an atheists' society making its members speak according to "Robert's Rules.") Robert's Rules of Order have become the standard for the orderly conduct of governing boards and other deliberative bodies.

HOW MUCH

Every group needs some rules of order. However, the rules needed depend on the number of members and the type of group. It is logical that a small group with clear goals needs fewer rules than a large group with confused goals. Yet the small group does need some rules to ensure that all persons

---

[1]M. B. Wheeler et al., *Basic Meeting Manual* (Nashville: Nelson, 1986), 60.

be heard. The large group needs more rules to keep moving and stay focused.

Often small groups (two to ten members) operate with only a few rules. They work like this: Someone raises a problem. Someone suggests a solution. They discuss and modify the suggestion. After the talk pauses, the chair asks if that is what the group wants. Everyone nods. Someone says, "Good! Now that that's over, let's go home." Everyone nods agreement, says good-bye, and leaves.

This group is operating under rules even though it may not look like it. The members talked about options and took a loose vote. No one moved a formal ending. But there was a ritual of sorts. This ritual gave members a chance to bring up other topics. Often groups operate in this loose manner for easy matters and slip into more formal methods when the issue is complex.

This is the way it goes: A problem comes before the group. Someone suggests a solution. A few people talk for it. Others talk against the suggestion. The talk goes back and forth, pro and con. A few make minor changes in the solution. A mild confusion level arises on exactly what is the solution being discussed. To deal with the rising frustration, someone makes a motion. Without any thought the group begins to operate with higher-level rules. By the meeting's end the group may have formally voted only half the decisions.

Medium-sized groups (eleven to thirty people) may use the main motion rules, but ignore using motions for adjournment or "calling the question" unless they are dealing with very disputed issues. Then they will use all the rules.

Larger groups (above thirty) may always use the complete rules. Expecting all groups regardless of size and function to use all the rules all the time is wrong. Any group can shift to more formal rules when needed.

MOTIONS

The rules of order focus on the agenda and motions. Agendas were covered in an earlier chapter. Here we will focus on motions.

Motions are the tools that drive the group through the agenda. There are twenty-seven types of motions, though in most meetings only a few are needed. For example, only the largest conventions would hear, "I rise to a question of privilege"—the motion used in emergencies. But even in small commitees we might hear, "I move . . ."

Knowing the different motions will help your meetings. You need to know these things about each type of motion: (1) What is the motion's purpose? (2) What are the words to say when making the motion? (3) When is making the motion proper? (4) Is a second required? (5) Can we debate the motion? (6) Can it be amended? (7) What vote is required (that is, majority, two-thirds, plurality, none)? (8) May the motion be reconsidered? Appendix 1 offers the different motions and answers these questions.

Typical Procedure

Here is a common procedure for conducting business in a meeting:

1. Someone presents a problem to the group.
2. The group discusses some options and finds out more about the problem. Light begins to shine on a possible solution.
3. Someone makes a main motion. Another person seconds the motion.
4. The chair calls for debate (discussion) on the motion.
5. The motion is debated.
6. Someone moves to amend the main motion. Someone seconds the amending motion.
7. The chair calls for debate on the amendment.
8. The amending motion is debated.
9. There is a vote on the amending motion. (For our purposes here, we will assume that the amendment was approved.)
10. You again discuss the main motion.
11. The chair calls for a vote on the main motion as amended.
12. There is a vote on the main motion.

This basic process is full of rules and customs, which can be confusing to the inexperienced committee member.

Main Motions

Main motions are Robert's workhorse. They are the tools that lead to solving problems. Make a main motion only when there is no other motion on the floor. It should be carefully worded and stated in positive terms. This is a negative motion: "I move that we don't let the Boy Scouts go camping." So voting against the camping trip requires a yea vote—a confusing situation. A better-worded motion would say, "I move that the Boy Scouts stay home." Now it is clearer what a yea or a no vote means.

This is another poorly worded motion: "I move that the church spend some money to take care of the needy." This gives the treasurer very little help: How much money? Which needy?

Try to write out a motion before you make it. It is amazing how awkward it is to state a motion aloud that seemed simple in your mind. Writing out the motion also helps the secretary record it in the minutes correctly.

After someone makes a motion and someone else seconds it, the chair restates the motion. Once the chair restates the motion, it can only be changed by a motion to amend. The motion's maker does not own the motion and can only amend it the way anyone else can.

No other main motions can be made while a main motion is on the floor, though amending motions are allowed. Members must vote on the main motion, requiring a majority vote, before another main motion can be made.

Amendments

The proper wording to amend a motion is this: "I move to amend the motion by . . ." After someone makes a motion to amend, rules limit debate to the amending motion. You cannot discuss the main motion or make another motion until the amending motion has been voted upon.

There are four forms of amendment:

111

1. Strike out certain consecutive words in the main motion.
2. Insert consecutive words in the main motion.
3. Strike out and insert consecutive words.
4. Append words to the end.

Notice the word *consecutive* in the list. Handling consecutive details averts having confusing amendments with multiple points on the floor. Suppose someone makes the motion, "I move that the clerk search for a suitable fax machine and spend up to five hundred dollars on it."

This would be an improper amendment: "I move to amend the motion by using the minister instead of the clerk and spending four hundred dollars instead of five hundred dollars."

This kind of multiple-point amendment confuses and complicates matters. It also opens the door to unfair actions. Some may favor the minister's buying the fax machine, but prefer the larger limit. Others may want the lower limit, but feel that the clerk should make the purchase. The mover should offer the changes in separate amendments. Making them together is confusing and creates a place where unfair actions are easy.

Amendments to amendments are acceptable. The idea seems simple, but managing it is tough. Suppose there is a main motion on the floor: "I move that we send every member a letter soliciting contributions to the building fund."

Now someone offers, "I move that we amend the motion by replacing the word 'member' with 'attending member and attending nonmember.'" The reason for the amendment is that the mover opposes asking nonattending members for money, but favors asking for donations from nonmembers who are regular attenders.

Debate is restricted to the specific subject of the amendment. In this case, the subject is who should receive the letter. It is not allowable at this point to discuss whether or not there should be a letter; the only proper issue is deciding to whom the letter would be sent.

Someone opposes sending it to nonmembers and says, "I move that we amend the amendment by striking 'and attending nonmembers.'"

Now the debate is limited to the question whether nonmembers should receive the letter. So talking about sending it to nonattending members is improper at the moment.

Compounding amendments requires an alert chair who properly controls the debate. It helps if the chair occasionally repeats the current motion: "The amendment before us is whether to strike the words 'to attending nonmembers.'"

Making amendments to amendments made to amendments and so forth is lawful. However, as the apostle Paul reminds us, all things may be lawful, but not all things are profitable. A wise chair will not let amending go too far. It would be more efficient to send the issue to a subcommittee to work out the wording.

After ample debate of the amendment to amend, the chair calls for a vote: "The vote before us is to strike the words 'to attending nonmembers.' A yea vote is for not sending it to nonmembers. A no vote means you favor sending it to nonmembers. All who approve of the amendment say yea. All opposed say no."

Suppose the amendment to the amendment passes. The chair says, "We are now discussing the amendment to replace the word 'member' with the words 'attending member.' Is there any discussion?" When discussion stops, the chair says, "Hearing no further discussion, I call for the vote on the amendment replacing the word 'member' with the words 'attending member.' If you favor sending the letter only to attending members, vote yea. If you favor sending it to all members regardless, vote no. All who favor the amendment say yea. All opposed to the amendment say no."

Suppose the amendment passes. The chair says, "We are now dealing with the main motion that we send every *attending* member a letter and ask each one to give to the building fund. Is there any discussion?"

Now those who oppose sending any letter at all can speak against the motion. After a while the chair repeats the motion and calls for the vote. Then the main motion is voted. As you can see, the amending process is complicated, but it is crucial to helping a committee take the best action and solve a problem satisfactorily.

Motions with Blanks

Motions can be made with blanks—that is, words omitted to be filled in later. This may seem strange, but this rule is helpful. Suppose the issue is recarpeting the church. A proper motion would be "I move that Joyce select a carpet and spend up to *blank* dollars for it." This motion expresses a desire to replace the carpet, but indicates that the mover is not sure of the cost.

Use a blank motion when a certain action is desired, but important details are missing or can be added subsequently without detriment. To fill in the blank, someone must offer an amendment to the motion.

In our example, the treasurer might say, "I move amending the motion by replacing the blank with six thousand dollars." The committee now discusses the amendment and votes the amount. Then it discusses the main motion and votes.

VOTING

Most motions pass with a majority of votes cast. On a tie vote a motion fails. The chair cannot vote except to break a tie or to make a tie, so his or her vote has great consequences. Suppose those favoring a motion are winning by one vote. The chair can vote for the other side and thereby force a tie— so the motion fails.

Sometimes a motion requires a two-thirds vote. There is an easy way to remember whether a majority or a two-thirds vote is needed. A two-thirds vote is necessary if the motion limits a person's rights as a committee member. For example, making nominations from the floor is a member's right. So a motion to close nominations requires a two-thirds vote. A motion to call the question requires a two-thirds vote, because it cuts off a member's right to discuss the issue. Voting for main motions and amendments does not usually affect a member's rights and require only a majority vote.

The chair calls, "All in favor say aye. All opposed say no"—this is called a voice vote. The chair decides the vote according to how many voices he or she heard each time. That is, if the chair judges the number of ayes, according to the volume, to exceed the number of nays, the motion passes. This is fine for votes requiring a majority vote, but for votes needing a two-thirds vote there must be an actual count, because the chair cannot discern two-thirds by ear.

Any member can question the chair's opinion of the vote by "calling for a division." This is common on close votes. After the chair announces the decision on a vote, anyone may say, "I call for a division." The chair says, "A division has been called. Those favoring the motion raise your hand [or stand]." The chair counts the votes favoring the action. Then the chair follows the same procedure with those opposed.

Time Limits and Calling the Question

Fairness entitles everyone to discuss the question, but large groups usually have a time limit on debate. Robert's Rules of Order limits debate to one ten-minute speech until everyone has had a turn; then it allows each another ten-minute speech. This rule applies only if the group does not have its own rules on debate. Usually small groups do not set limits.

The rules ensure that everyone has an equal chance to discuss the issue. These rules in turn are subject to two actions: (1) a motion to extend debate, and (2) calling the question.

A motion to extend debate beyond the set time limit requires a majority vote. It is used when everyone has had a time or turn to speak but the group favors letting the debate continue. This action is obviously more likely to come in large groups than in small ones.

The most misused rule is "calling the question." The formal name is to "move the previous question." This is the way it works: There is a main motion on the floor. Someone may feel that the debate has gone on long enough. That person must be recognized by the chair and state, "I move the question." This motion must be seconded. There is no debate, and the motion requires a two-thirds vote to pass.

Shouting out "Question" and expecting that to end the debate happens often, but it is rude. That practice runs contrary to the spirit of the rules of order.

Dividing the Question

A motion to divide the question is useful if a problem is complex. This motion cannot be debated, and it requires a majority vote. This is how it works: Suppose there is a motion to set up a fund-raising subcommittee and send a letter to every member soliciting donations to the building program."

A person favoring the subcommittee but opposing the letter says, "I move to divide the question." If there is a second, the chair, without allowing debate, declares, "There has been a motion to divide the question. All in favor of dividing the question say aye. All opposed say no." If the motion carries, then the original motion has become two: one to establish the subcommittee; the other, to send a letter.

Elections and Secret Ballots

Managing elections can be tricky. Seeking not to offend anyone and trying to maintain a good working relationship among members are important objectives. Elections involve strong feelings, so they can readily trigger parliamentary abuses. And electing the best person without hurting the losers' feelings is difficult.

For these reasons, a group's bylaws often specify its election rules. Typically in large groups, a nominating committee prepares a slate of candidates. At the election meeting, the nominating committee makes the initial nominations. Then the chair calls for nominations from the floor. The chair continues to accept nominations from the floor until there are no more forthcoming or until a motion to close nominations (a motion requiring a two-thirds vote) is passed.

After the nominations close, the chair calls for discussion of the candidates. Rule books do not require that candidates leave the room during this discussion or during the voting; but most groups practice the custom of excusing the candidates at least from discussion.

Then the chair supervises the voting process. The group's bylaws should specify whether someone needs a majority or a plurality vote to win. A majority is when more than half the votes are cast for one person. A plurality is when one person has most of the votes, but not a majority. Plurality votes apply only when there are more than two candidates.

Suppose one hundred members cast votes. The bylaws say that a person needs a majority to win an election—in this case, at least fifty-one votes. If the rules say a plurality is needed, then the candidate with the most votes wins. If there are three candidates, one could win with as few as thirty-four votes; the other two would gain no more than thirty-three apiece.

When there are more than two candidates and a majority vote is required, it is common that no one will be elected on the first ballot. Obviously it is possible that there could be many ballots without one candidate's achieving a majority of the votes. Therefore some procedure must be applied that reduces the number of candidates and increases the probability of one candidate's receiving a majority. This usually means removing the lower vote-getters from the ballot and retaining only the top two. This phenomenon is familiar at the national conventions of political parties, where "favorite son" candidates are nominated for President of the United States with no realistic chance of winning, but with an opportunity to affect strategy and exert influence on the eventual outcome.

Secret Ballots

Bylaws often require secret ballots for elections or other designated actions. Even when secret ballots are not required, members will ask for them when voting on sensitive issues to avoid hurting the colleagues' feelings. However, going through several secret ballots trying to achieve a majority can be very tiresome.

Suppose there are nine candidates for a position. The members write their three favorites on a paper, and someone tallies the votes. Usually the members wait during this count and do not conduct any other business. Then they take another vote with a reduced slate comprising the three who recieved the most votes on the first ballot. The votes are tallied again, and the members wait again and so on until someone is elected.

Procedures that allow voting for more than one candidate—as in the preceding example—can make the process tedious. Nor does this procedure ensure electing the best person for the job. Despite these drawbacks, however, many groups like to proceed that way.

Baptizing the Election Process

Handling discussions and elections in a Christian way can be difficult. Discussing the candidate's strengths and weaknesses in a public forum can open the door to abuse. Some churches handle this sensitive problem by allowing members to send a nomination back to the nominating committee, thereby indicating a question about the nominee's qualifications. A member doing this will then meet with the nominating committee to explain why there is a problem with that candidate. The nominating committee will decide whether there is merit to the complaint. Eventually the nominating committee will bring to the full group a modified slate.

This process bars nominations from the floor. It is not entirely the fairest process, but it averts having to discuss a nominee's character in an open meeting.

POINTS OF ORDER

Often there are problems with the way the chair is applying the rules of order. Should you feel that the chair is being unfair in procedures, you may declare, "I rise to a point of order." This can occur at any time, even interrupting the current speaker.

In response, the chair says, "State your point."

Then we state what rule we believe the chair has violated—for example, "Calling the question requires a two-thirds vote" or "You are unfairly calling only on those who favor the motion."

The chair may reply, "The speaker is correct. Calling the question does require a two-thirds vote. The motion calling the question is lost" or "The speaker is incorrect. I am calling people according to when they raised their hands to speak."

If we do not agree with the chair's ruling, we may make a motion to appeal. This is a motion that brings the chair's decision to a vote by the entire group. It may be debated, and it requires a majority vote.

Points of order may deal with rude conduct in the group that we feel the chair should straighten out.

People sometimes misuse points of order—to gain attention or perhaps to interrupt a particular speaker. Then instead of stating a problem with the process, they give an argument in the current debate. The chair must not allow this kind of misuse to continue.

Rules of order are useful tools to guide a group through the decision-making process. Bogging down the process by rigorously applying the rules runs contrary to their purpose. Each group should agree on the rules they feel are needed in their situation.

Conclusion

Now that you have read this book, what will be different about your meetings? Following is a summary of important points we have covered. I suggest you choose a few and work to apply them in your forthcoming meetings. Return to the list in a few months and select a few more. Apply them to yourself, saying, "I will . . ."

1. Seek how Christian committees exist to find God's will.
2. Practice making people more important than meetings.
3. Consider eliminating certain meetings and letting individuals make the decisions.
4. Spend time thinking about whether my committee is the right type for its purpose.
5. Review the organization's committees to ensure that each one is the right size for its function.
6. Begin stating each meeting's purpose clearly.
7. Put thought into the meeting place.
8. Put special effort into compiling the agenda. Consider changing from the timeworn "old business/new business" format.
9. Include "discussion only" agenda items in each meeting.
10. Clarify my role as servant-leader in meetings.

11. Improve the management of meeting details (that is, agenda, announcements, thank-you notes, and so on.
12. Consider allowing other kinds of people to chair the committees (for example, nonofficers in place of officers).
13. Clarify my role as a servant when doing committee work.
14. Assist the chair in leading the group to decisions.
15. Prepare for the meetings in which I am a member.
16. Support the committee's decisions outside the meeting room.
17. Work to build ownership of the committee actions.
18. Handle follow-up work more carefully.
19. Look for a way to improve the committee's minutes.
20. Begin evaluating meetings.
21. Begin evaluating decisions.
22. Review the committee for game playing and try to reduce the number of games I play.
23. Review the committee for groupthink and try applying some of the remedies.
24. Look at the rules of order established for the committee. Make sure they are not used hurtfully.
25. Look at the group's election process. Is it fair, and does it protect church unity?

PASTOR JIM

Pastor Jim is alive and well. He took a position in a larger church. He did not like it. By all reports, he did a fine job there, but he missed Shulerville. He stayed at the new church for about a year and then returned to Shulerville. Brother Ebenezer was glad to see him come back—at least in his own way he was glad. Ebenezer said, "Anything is better than that—" Well, take my word for it, he is glad to have Jim back. And Jim is glad to be back.

Privileged Motions

MOTION	PURPOSE	FORM	INTERRUPT SPEAKER?	SECOND REQUIRED?	DEBATABLE?	AMENDABLE?	REQUIRED VOTE	CAN RECONSIDER
Fix the time to adjourn	Set time to continue meeting	"I move that we adjourn to meet at . . ."	No	Yes	No	Yes	Majority	Yes
Adjourn	End meeting	"I move that we adjourn."	No	Yes	No	No	Majority	No
Recess	Provide break	"I move a ten-minute recess."	No	Yes	No	Yes	Majority	No
Question of privilege	Obtain action immediately in an emergency	"I rise to a question of privilege."	Yes	No	No	No	None	No
Orders of the day	Demand the group stick to the agenda	"I call for the orders of the day."	Yes	No	No	No	None	No

122

Subsidiary Motions

MOTION	PURPOSE	FORM	INTERRUPT SPEAKER?	SECOND REQUIRED?	DEBATABLE?	AMENDABLE?	REQUIRED VOTE	CAN RECONSIDER
Lay a question on the table	Set aside for more vital business	"I move to table the motion."	No	Yes	No	No	Majority	No
Previous question	Stop debate	"I move the previous question."	No	Yes	No	No	2/3	No
Limit or extend limits on debate	Regulate debate	"I move the debate be limited to . ."	No	Yes	No	Yes	2/3	Yes
Postpone definitely	Delay action to a specific time	"I move that we postpone action to . "	No	Yes	Yes	Yes	Majority	Yes
Postpone indefinitely	Kill a motion without bringing it to a vote	"I move the matter be postponed"	No	Yes	Yes	No	Majority	Yes
Commit or recommit	Place question in a committee's hands	"I move that we refer this matter to . ."	No	Yes	Yes	Yes	Majority	Yes
Amend	Change or modify a motion	"I move to amend by . . ."	No	Yes	Yes	Yes	Majority	Yes
Main motion	Introduce new business	"I move that . . ."	No	Yes	Yes	Yes	Majority	Yes

Incidental Motions

MOTION	PURPOSE	FORM	INTERRUPT SPEAKER?	SECOND REQUIRED?	DEBATABLE?	AMENDABLE?	VOTE REQUIRED	CAN RECONSIDER
Point of order	Enforce the rules	"I rise to a point of order."	Yes	No	No	No	None	No
Appeal	Reverse the chair's decision	"I appeal the decision of the chair."	Yes	Yes	Yes	No	Majority negative	Yes
Suspend a rule	Allow action contrary to the rules	"I move to suspend the rules."	No	Yes	No	No	2/3	No
Objection to consideration of a motion	Avoid discussion of a question	"I object to the consideration of this motion."	No	No	No	Yes	Majority	No
Divide the question	Consider one item at a time	"I move to divide the question."	No	No	No	Yes	Majority	No
Consideration seriatim	Perfect each paragraph before voting	"I move to consider the question seriatim."	No	Yes	No	No	Majority	No
Division of the group	Verify an announced vote	"I call for the division of the group."	Yes	No	No	No	None	No

124

Incidental Motions (continued)

MOTION	PURPOSE	FORM	INTERRUPT SPEAKER?	SECOND REQUIRED?	DEBATABLE?	AMENDABLE?	VOTE REQUIRED	CAN RECONSIDER
Relating to nominations	End nominations	"I move that nominations be closed."	No	Yes	No	No	2/3	No
Parliamentary inquiry and point of information	Provide parliamentary and other information	"I rise to a parliamentary inquiry."	Yes	No	No	No	None	No
Withdraw or modify a motion	Withdraw a motion before it is voted	"I request permission to withdraw my motion."	No	No	No	No	None	No
Take from the table[1]	Bring up a motion previously tabled	"I move the motion be taken from the table."	No	Yes	No	No	Majority	No
Reconsider[1]	Try to get a second vote	"I move to reconsider . . ."	Yes	Yes	Yes	No	Majority	No
Rescind[1]	Void or repeal a past motion	"I move that we rescind the action . . ."	No	Yes	Yes	Yes	Majority[2]	Yes
Ratify[1]	Make valid action already taken	"I move that . . ."	No	Yes	Yes	Yes	Majority	Yes

1. Out of order if another motion is on the floor.
2. Requires a majority if there is a notice before the meeting. Otherwise this requires a two-thirds vote.